Instant Lessons ❶

Elementary

Deirdre Howard-Williams
Mary Tomalin
Peter Watcyn-Jones
Edward Woods

Series Editor:
Peter Watcyn-Jones

PENGUIN ENGLISH

Pearson Education Limited
Edinburgh Gate
Harlow
Essex CM20 2JE, England
and Associated Companies throughout the world.

ISBN 0 582 42783 5

First published 2000
Copyright © Deirdre Howard-Williams, Mary Tomalin, Peter Watcyn-Jones, Edward Woods 2000

The moral right of the authors has been asserted.

Every effort has been made to trace the copyright holders in every case. The publishers would be interested to hear from any not acknowledged.

Designed by Ferdinand Pageworks
Typeset by Pantek Arts
Illustrations by Sir Vin, Chris Pavely and Pantek Arts
Printed in Spain by Mateu Cromo S.A., Pinto, Madrid

All rights reserved; no part of this publication may be reproduced, stored in a retrieval system, or transmitted in any form or by any means, electronic, mechanical, photocopying, recording or otherwise, without the prior written permission of the Publishers.

Photocopying notice
The pages in this book marked From *Instant Lessons 1 Elementary* edited by Peter Watcyn-Jones © Penguin Books 2000 **Photocopiable** may be photocopied free of charge for classroom use by the purchasing individual or institution. This permission to copy does not extend to branches or additional schools of an institution. All other copying is subject to permission from the publisher.

Acknowledgements
The publishers make grateful acknowledgement for permission to reproduce the following photographs:
p 15, 'Lock at Bourgival, France, 1956', Henri Cartier-Bresson/Magnum Photos; p 17, 'Lamego, Beira Alta, Portugal, 1955', Henri Cartier-Bresson/Magnum Photos; p 63, Robert de Niro and Arnold Schwarzenegger, Rex Features Ltd

Published by Pearson Education Limited in association with Penguin Books Ltd, both companies being subsidiaries of Pearson plc.

For a complete list of the titles available from Penguin English please visit our website at www.penguinenglish.com, or write to your local Pearson Education office or to: Marketing Department, Penguin Longman Publishing, 5 Bentinck Street, London W1U 2EG.

Contents

Reading by Mary Tomalin

		page
1	Au pair	6
2	Holiday	10
3	Photographs	14
4	I didn't do it!	18
5	Health	22
6	The lottery ticket	26
7	How do you sleep?	30
8	Help!	32
9	A new life	36
10	Postcards	40

Grammar by Edward Woods

		page
21	Present Simple	64
22	Present Simple: interrogative and negative forms	68
23	The article	72
24	*Some/any* and countable/uncountable	76
25	Past Simple v Past Continuous	78
26	Frequency adverbs	82
27	Prepositions of time	86
28	Prepositions of place	88
29	Adverbs	94
30	Demonstratives and possessives	96

Writing by Deirdre Howard-Williams

11	Consequences	44
12	Four easy steps	46
13	World weather reports	48
14	Food for thought	50
15	My ideal penfriend	52
16	Advice from Anna	54
17	Colours	56
18	An English weekend	58
19	The last chocolate cake	60
20	Trip to the top	62

Vocabulary by Peter Watcyn-Jones

31	Clothes	100
32	*Foot + ball = football*	104
33	The living room	108
34	Countries and nationalities	112
35	What do they look like?	114
36	Food	118
37	Useful adjectives	120
38	The family	122
39	Shops and shopping	124
40	Verb + noun collocations	126

Introduction

Instant Lessons 1 Elementary is the first in a new series of photocopiable resource books for teachers and contains 40 complete lessons for practising reading, writing, grammar and vocabulary. It is aimed at busy teachers who need an 'instant' or ready-made lesson. Although it is intended primarily for teachers new to the profession and non-native-speaking teachers, even the more experienced teacher should find a lot that is useful in the book.

Each activity contains material to be photocopied, usually one sheet or two, and clear step-by-step instructions to the teacher on preparation and organization. **Instant Lessons 1 Elementary** can be used with adults and teenagers in a variety of different class situations to give extra practice in reading, writing, grammar and vocabulary in a fun and stimulating way.

Most of the lessons involve the students working in pairs or in small groups, which is an excellent way of making the learning process more dynamic and enjoyable.

Instant Lessons 1 Elementary is not meant to replace a coursebook but is intended as a useful resource book to compliment any existing coursebook at this level. The teacher can simply pick and choose from it according to how useful and interesting a particular lesson is to his/her class.

How to use this book

Instant Lessons 1 Elementary contains forty lessons. These are divided into four main sections:
Reading
Writing
Grammar
Vocabulary
with ten lessons per section.

Each lesson is complete in itself and consists of teacher's notes, a key (where appropriate) and one or more handout. Each lesson is intended to take 50–55 minutes and the very detailed teacher's notes give clear guidance on how many minutes each part of the lesson might take. There is also a comprehensive key, which again makes life a lot easier for the busy teacher. Finally, the teacher's notes are deliberately placed together with the handouts and, where possible, as a two-page spread – again to make the book 'user-friendly' and easy to teach from.

Choosing a lesson for your class

Lesson type
The teacher's notes for each lesson show at a glance the main teaching point of the lesson, making it a fairly easy task to find a suitable lesson to use quickly. The lessons are all at elementary level and do not need to be done in sequence as each lesson is complete in itself. However, there is a slight progression in the level of difficulty, with the slightly easier lessons coming at the beginning of each section.

Preparing the activity before the lesson
The teacher's notes to each activity have a special section called *Preparation*. This section tells you exactly what you need to do before the class starts, i.e. how many pages to photocopy, how many copies are needed and if the copies need to be cut up in any way.

Organizing the activity in the classroom

Lesson plan
The teacher's notes for each lesson in **Instant Lessons 1 Elementary** are divided into four main parts:
Introduction
Presentation
Practice
Conclusion
In addition, there is usually a section at the end with suggestions for homework.

Introduction
The teacher's notes start with suggestions as to how to introduce each activity. It is usually short – no more than 5 minutes.

Presentation
This is where the main teaching point is presented. It is nearly always teacher-led. It varies in length between 15 and 20 minutes.

Practice
This is always student-centred and is where the students get a chance to practise, where possible in a communicative way, what they have been taught in the previous section. Students normally work in pairs or groups. This is usually the longest part of the lesson (approximately 20–25 minutes).

Teacher's notes

Conclusion
Like the introduction, each lesson has a short activity at the end (5 minutes) to round it off. It is often used as a quick check to see if the students have assimilated the main points of the lesson.

Pair and group work
In most lessons students will spend much of their time working in pairs or groups. As such, a certain amount of classroom reorganization may be needed.

Where possible, rearrange the classroom slightly to make it easier for students to work in pairs or groups without disturbing others. Where this is not possible, students doing pairwork should work with the person sitting beside them or the person in front or behind (they just need to turn round). For group work, two students can easily turn their chairs round to face two others behind them. When you have an uneven number of students, most pair activities can be done by three people (if necessary, two students against one).

As far as possible, vary the pairs and groups so that students do not always work with the same people. It can sometimes be useful, for example, to mix stronger and weaker students in a small group so that they can help one another.

The enormous advantage of working in pairs and groups is that it gives everyone a chance to speak and in a non-threatening environment, i.e. with a fellow-student rather than in front of the teacher and the whole class. Students will learn from one another in a natural way that approximates more to the world outside and gets away from some of the constraints of the classroom. If this type of activity is new to them, it is useful to explain its advantages and to encourage them to take full advantage by participating as much as they can and sticking strictly to English!

The role of the teacher while this is going on is to facilitate communication by walking round the classroom, pausing briefly beside each pair/group. If all is going well, just encourage and move on. If things are not going so well, offer help and encouragement as needed to get students working well together.

While walking round, it is useful to have a small notebook or piece of paper on which you note down any common problems or persistent mistakes you hear. You can discuss these with the whole class during the feedback session – it is usually better to avoid saying who made each mistake as this can have a discouraging effect!

A note about photocopying

Since this is a photocopiable book with each activity containing one or more handout, it may be worth looking at ways of reducing the costs – both in terms of time and money. The material to be photocopied can be divided into two types: (a) handouts which the students write on, and (b) material which the students use but do not write on. Of the latter, many are cut up into cards.

For material that can be re-used, wherever possible try mounting it on cards and protecting it either by laminating it or (a cheaper solution) by keeping it in clear plastic folders. The extra initial effort will certainly pay off as subsequent photocopying costs and time will be reduced greatly.

Reading: Lessons 1–10

1 Au pair

Aim	To understand job advertisement and letters offering work.
Preparation	Copy the handouts on pages 7 and 9 – one copy per student.

Introduction *(5 minutes)*

Write the word *au pair* on the board. Check students understand the word (an au pair is a young person, usually a woman, who stays with a family in a foreign country and looks after their children). Ask students to give you as many words and phrases as they can think of connected with au pairs. For example: *language classes, children, family, housework, foreign country, lonely, not much money*. Write their ideas on the board.

Presentation *(20 minutes)*

Activity A In pairs, students read the text and answer the questions. Encourage students to use dictionaries where necessary. Check answers orally, explaining where necessary. Correct major errors.

Activity B Elicit/pre-teach *advertisement*. Students read the advertisements, using dictionaries where necessary. Then they complete the chart. Walk round, giving help and encouragement. Then check orally. Write new words on the board in sentences.

(continued on page 8)

Key

A 1 Age: 18
Nationality: Spanish
City: Madrid
2 Because she wants to learn to speak good English, and also because she likes children.

B

	City	No. of children	Babies (under 2)	Hours work a day	Car	Pay
a	✔	3	✗	6	✗	£70
b	✗	3	✗	10	✔	£80
c	✗	2	✔	5	✗	£65
d	✔	2	✗	6	✔	£70

(continued on page 8)

Teacher's notes

1 Au pair

A Work in pairs. Read this, then answer the questions below.

Amaya is an eighteen-year-old Spanish girl from Madrid. She wants to work in hotels in Spain. Her English isn't very good and she knows it must be good for a hotel job. She has decided to work as an au pair for a year in England because this will help her English. She likes children (but not babies) and wants to be in a big city.

1 Complete this information about Amaya.

```
Age:
Nationality:
City:
```

2 Why does Amaya want to work as an au pair?

B A family friend sends these advertisements from England. Work in pairs. Read them and complete the chart below.

a CENTRAL LONDON
Au pair wanted for friendly family with boy and 2 girls, 8, 13 and 14. Six hours work 5 days a week. Central London. Very good language school nearby. £70 a week.

b Au Pair – £80 per week
Wanted. Au pair for single working mother with three children, two, five and nine. Working hours 8.00–6.00 Monday–Friday. £80 per week. Country town. Use of car.

c Au pair wanted for happy family with two boys aged two and six months. Five hours work a day, 3 evenings. Seaside town. £65 a week.

d Loving family needs friendly au pair for 2 boys, 5 and 6. Six hours work 5 days a week. Own car. Near central London. £70 a week.

	City	No. of children	Babies (under 2)	Hours work a day	Car	Pay
a		3	✗			£
b	✗					£
c				5		£
d					✓	£70

(✓ = yes ✗ = no)

From *Instant Lessons 1 Elementary* edited by Peter Watcyn-Jones © Penguin Books 2000

Teacher's notes

Practice (25 minutes)

Activity C Elicit/pre-teach *to be interested in*. In pairs, students discuss the questions. Elicit answers orally and ask students to explain what is wrong with the other two families. You may want to write up the answers on the board. For example:
Amaya is interested in advertisement a because the family is in London. There are no babies in the family. There is a good language school nearby.

Activity D In pairs or small groups, the students read the letters and answer questions 1 and 2. Students use their dictionaries where necessary. Check answers orally, explaining where necessary. Correct major errors. An example answer to question 2 might be:
The family in letter 1 do not sound very friendly. They want to leave Amaya alone at weekends! Also, they want her to speak Spanish every day, which will not be good for her English. Family 2 sound much nicer. They want to help Amaya with her English and say she will be 'one of the family'.
Write new words on the board in sentences.

Activity E In pairs, students find the words in the text. **Omit if lack of time.**

Activity F Walk round and listen to students as they discuss this question. Listen to their mistakes and briefly go through the mistakes. Then elicit answers from each group. **Omit if lack of time.**

Conclusion (5 minutes)

Ask the students to choose three new words they have learnt in the lesson and to write a sentence using each of them. Walk round and check the sentences. **Omit if lack of time.**

Homework

Written answer to Activity D, question 2. Also Activity E, if not done in class.

Key

C Amaya will be interested in advertisements a and d. She will be interested in advertisement a because the family is in London. They say they are friendly. There are no babies in the family and there's a good language school nearby. The hours of work are not too long and the money (£70 a week) is all right. She will be interested in family d for the same reasons. The family does not say that there is a good language school nearby but she is near the centre of London and she will have her own car. She can find a good language school.
Amaya will not be interested in advertisement b because ten hours a day is too long. Also the job is in a town, not a city. She will not be interested in advertisement c because it is not in a city and the family has a small baby.

D 1 Letter 1/advertisment a. The writer talks about two girls.
Letter 2/advertisment d. The writer talks about two boys.
2 *Possible answer:* Amaya will choose the family in letter 2. The family in letter 1 do not sound very friendly. They want to leave Amaya alone at weekends! Also, they want her to speak Spanish every day – this will not be good for her English. The family in letter 2 sound much nicer. They want to help Amaya with her English and say she will be 'one of the family'.

E 1 ... you will have our London house to yourself!
2 Paul ... already loves reading ...
3 We were very happy to hear from you.
4 We will do our best to help you.
5 At weekends we go away ...
6 Here are some photographs of my husband and me and the boys.

1 Au pair *(continued)*

C Which advertisements do you think Amaya will be interested in? Why? What's wrong with the others?

D Amaya writes to two of the families and they write back to her. Work in pairs or small groups. Answer these questions.

1 Read the two letters and then say which advertisements (a, b, c or d) they go with.

2 Which family do you think Amaya will choose? Why?

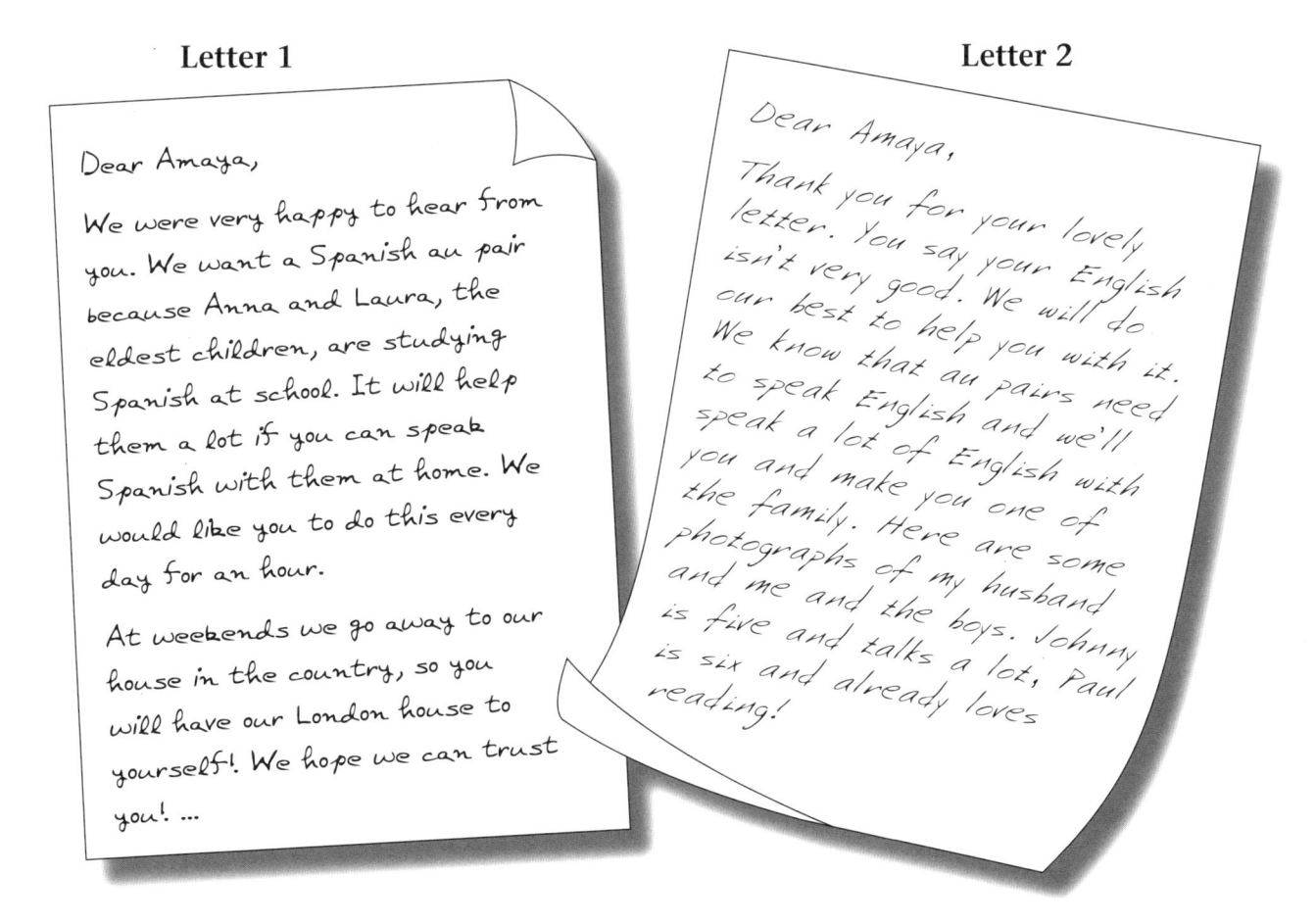

Letter 1

Dear Amaya,

We were very happy to hear from you. We want a Spanish au pair because Anna and Laura, the eldest children, are studying Spanish at school. It will help them a lot if you can speak Spanish with them at home. We would like you to do this every day for an hour.

At weekends we go away to our house in the country, so you will have our London house to yourself! We hope we can trust you! ...

Letter 2

Dear Amaya,

Thank you for your lovely letter. You say your English isn't very good. We will do our best to help you with it. We know that au pairs need to speak English and we'll speak a lot of English with you and make you one of the family. Here are some photographs of my husband and me and the boys. Johnny is five and talks a lot, Paul is six and already loves reading!

E Work in pairs. Read the letters again. Which words in the letters mean the same as these words?

1 You will be alone in the house.

2 He likes books a lot.

3 It was nice to get your letter.

4 We will try to help you.

5 From Friday until Sunday we go away.

6 These are pictures of our family.

F Work in pairs. Would you like to work as an au pair? Say why/why not.

From *Instant Lessons 1 Elementary* edited by Peter Watcyn-Jones © Penguin Books 2000

Teacher's notes

2 Holiday

Aim	To compare two people's accounts of the same holiday.
Preparation	Copy the handouts on pages 11 and 13 – one copy per student.

Introduction *(5 minutes)*

In pairs, students look at the pictures in Activity A. Ask: *Which place would you like to stay in for a holiday? Why?* Elicit answers from students.

Presentation *(10 minutes)*

Activity A Elicit/pre-teach the word *beach*. In pairs, the students read the text and look at the pictures. Question 1: Students say which apartment the writer stayed in. Tell the students not to use their dictionaries for this activity. Question 2: Students try and guess the meaning of the words from context. Check answers orally, explaining and helping students to guess the answers from the context.

Practice *(30 minutes)*

Activity B Pre-teach the word *relationship*. In pairs, students read the text in Activity A again and also the text in Activity B. They look at the pictures and answer the questions, using their dictionaries where necessary. Check answers orally, explaining where necessary.

(continued on page 12)

Key

A 1 He stayed in the apartment in picture 1. We know this because of the words: *There weren't too many people on the beach./It was good to be in an apartment and not some big, noisy hotel with people everywhere.*
   2 *clear:* not dirty; you can see to the bottom of the sea.
      noisy: with lots of noise, for example of people talking loudly.
      together: with each other.
      spent (to spend): stayed/were.

B The man, Mike, wrote the text in Activity A. The woman, Maria, wrote the text in Activity B. They are married with children.

(continued on page 12)

2 Holiday

A Work in pairs. Read the text and answer the questions.

1 The pictures show two apartments. Read the text. Which apartment did the writer stay in? How do you know?

2 Can you guess the meaning of the four underlined words (lines 4 and 8)?

Picture 1   Picture 2

It was a great holiday. The weather was good – really hot. The best thing was that our apartment was only 100 metres from the beach. I got up at eight every day and had a swim before breakfast. There weren't many people on the beach and the sea was blue and <u>clear</u>. The children were fine. It was good to be in an apartment and not some big,
5 <u>noisy</u> hotel with people everywhere. I travel a lot for my job, and stay in good hotels, so I don't want to stay in one when I'm on holiday. I don't even want to eat in restaurants much. I do too much of that when I travel. Maria and I did the cooking and shopping <u>together</u>, so that was all right. We <u>spent</u> most days on the beach. It was good to lie in the sun, get brown and play with the children. We were two miles from the
10 nearest village. That was good too. Good to be alone with the family for two weeks.

B Work in pairs. Read the text in Activity A again. Also, read the text opposite. Look at the pictures. Which person wrote text A? Which person wrote text B? What are their names? What is their relationship?

11 I enjoyed the holiday. It's a beautiful place and the food is wonderful. But it's too hot in August, so I didn't sleep well. And the baby woke me every night at about
15 four! Mike never went to him – it was always me. But the children were good and they loved being near the beach. So did I – it was wonderful! And the sea was so clear! But next time I want to stay in a hotel.
20 I'm tired of shopping and cooking every day. I don't think Mike understands that. He was very good and helped me with it, but I have to do it every day at home. He doesn't! Also, the nearest village was too
25 far away and there was almost no one on the beach. I like meeting people, but there was no one to meet! But it is a beautiful place. We'll go back next year and stay in a hotel in town. And we'll go in June when it's
30 not so hot.

From *Instant Lessons 1 Elementary* edited by Peter Watcyn-Jones © Penguin Books 2000

Teacher's notes

Activity C Students read both texts again. Check students understand the task. Go through the chart orally, asking students to predict the answers. Then, in pairs, students complete the chart. Walk round and check their answers.

Activity D Students read the questions. Check they understand them. Then, in pairs, students answer the questions. Check answers orally, explaining where necessary. Correct major errors. Encourage discussion for questions 3 and 5. Example language for question 3: *They are probably quite happy, but perhaps the man doesn't help the woman much with the baby. Why doesn't he get up at night sometimes?* For question 5, correct major errors. **Omit 1–3 if lack of time.**

Activity E Don't worry about grammar too much in students' answers. Just make sure they understand what the underlined words are referring to. **Omit if lack of time.**

Conclusion (5 minutes)

Activity F Students write one or two sentences about their best holiday. Elicit some model answers before students write. Walk round and check their sentences.

Homework

Students write a short paragraph about their best or worst holiday.

Key

C

	Woman	Man
The weather		
It was too hot.	✔	
I liked the weather.		✔
I didn't sleep very well.	✔	
Children and baby		
The children were fine.	✔	✔
The baby woke me every night.	✔	
Position of apartment		
I loved being near the beach.	✔	✔
It was too far to the nearest village.	✔	
I liked being two miles from the village.		✔
Cooking and shopping		
I didn't like cooking and shopping every day.	✔	
The cooking and shopping was OK.		✔

D 1 He travels a lot. He stays in good hotels and eats in restaurants.
  2 Because it won't be so hot in June.
  3 *Possible answer:* They are probably quite happy, but Maria would prefer Mike to help more with the baby. Why doesn't he get up at night sometimes? But at least he helped with the shopping and cooking on holiday. They don't communicate very well. Mike seems not to realize that Maria didn't like everything about the holiday.
  4 You can swim, get brown, play with your children, lie in the sun, play ball, walk along the beach, watch people, read, sleep.
  5 *Possible answer:* I'd prefer a holiday in a hotel. I don't want to cook or shop when I'm on holiday. And I don't want to clean. And you can meet people in a hotel – I'd like that.

E 1 a hotel
  2 eating in restaurants
  3 the baby
  4 being near the beach
  5 the shopping and cooking

2 Holiday (continued)

C Work in pairs. Read both texts again. The woman and the man feel differently about the holiday. Look at the sentences in this chart. Tick (✔) who says or feels these things, the man, the woman, or both.

	Woman	Man
The weather		
It was too hot.		
I liked the weather.		✔
I didn't sleep very well.		
Children and baby		
The children were fine.		
The baby woke me every night.		
Position of apartment		
I loved being near the beach.		
It was too far to the nearest village.		
I liked being two miles from the village.		
Cooking and shopping		
I didn't like cooking and shopping every day.		
The cooking and shopping was OK.		

D Work in pairs. Answer the questions.
1 What do we learn about the husband's job?
2 Why does the woman want to go back next year in June?
3 Do you think the man and the woman are happy together?
4 What can you do on a beach? Write down three things.
5 Which would you like better, a holiday in an apartment on a beach, or in a hotel on a beach? Say why.

E Work in pairs. What do the underlined words mean?
1 I don't want to stay in one when I'm on holiday. (line 6)
2 I do too much of that when I travel. (line 7)
3 Mike never went to him – it was always me. (line 15)
4 So did I – it was wonderful! (line 18)
5 He was very good and helped me with it. (line 23)

F Write one or two sentences about your best holiday.

Teacher's notes

3 Photographs

Aim	To match photographs to written descriptions.
Preparation	Copy the handouts on pages 15 and 17 – one copy per student.

Introduction (5 minutes)

Students look at the picture in Activity A. Ask them these questions: *Where are the women? What country do you think this is?* Possible answers to the first question: *They're on a boat./They're in the doorway of a boat. I think the boat is on a river or canal.* You may need to teach the word *canal* (and possibly *river* too) as not many students will know this. Teach the word *doorway* as students will probably want to use it. Possible answers to the second question: *Perhaps it's Spain or Portugal.* (In fact, it's Portugal.) Higher level: *It could be Spain or Portugal.*

Presentation (20 minutes)

Activity A Students look at the picture for one minute. Then, in pairs, they read the text and underline the mistakes. Encourage students to use their dictionaries. Then check answers orally, explaining where necessary. Ask students to correct the mistakes. Then students can study the picture.

Activity B In pairs or small groups, the students read the questions and use dictionaries if necessary. Then check they understand the questions. When they have discussed in pairs, have a whole class discussion. Example answer for question 1: *Because he's the woman's husband and the baby is his child. The woman and baby look very happy to see him.* Example answer for question 2: *I think he works outside because his shoulders and arms are bare.* Example answer for question 3: *Perhaps the older woman is the other woman's mother.* Correct major errors. Write new words on the board in sentences. **Omit questions 3 and 4 if lack of time.**

(continued on page 16)

Key

A ... he has <u>both</u> hands on his hips ... The baby has <u>nothing</u> on ... looking up at <u>the man/him</u> ... The dog is standing <u>near/over</u> some rope

B 1 *Possible answer:* Because he's the woman's husband and the baby is his child. The woman and baby look very happy to see him.
   2 His shoulders and arms are bare. I think he works outside.
   3 *Possible answer:* Perhaps they're friends. Or perhaps the older woman is the other woman's mother.
   4 b
   5 *Possible answer:* I feel good. The woman and child look happy. It's a happy picture.

(continued on page 16)

3 Photographs

A Work in pairs. Look at this picture for one minute.

There are some mistakes in this description of the picture. Find the mistakes.

A man is standing with his back to us – we can't see his face. His arms and shoulders are bare and he has one hand on his hips. He's looking down into the doorway of a boat. In the doorway there are two women, an older woman and a young woman. The young woman is holding a baby in her arms. The baby has a t-shirt on and is smiling at the man. The woman is wearing earrings and has bare feet. There's a dog between the two women. There's another dog near the man, looking up at the baby. The dog is standing on some rope.

B Work in pairs or small groups. Discuss these questions.

1 Why do you think the man is looking at the women and baby?

2 What kind of work do you think the man does? Why do you think this?

3 What do you think the relationship is between the two women?

4 Where do you think the boat is? **a** by the sea **b** on a canal **c** on a river?

5 How do you feel when you look at this picture? Can you say why you feel this?

From *Instant Lessons 1 Elementary* edited by Peter Watcyn-Jones © Penguin Books 2000   **Photocopiable**   15

Teacher's notes

Practice (20–25 minutes)

Activity C In pairs, the students look at the second picture. Then they read the two descriptions below it, and say which is the best description in their opinion. Allow use of dictionaries.
Description 1 says: *I don't think the man is the woman's husband.* Description 2 says: *The father is looking at his wife and children.* Explain there is no correct answer to this question. Encourage discussion. Correct major errors.

Activity D In pairs, the students read the questions. Check students understand the words *similar, both, show*. Elicit some answers from students and encourage discussion. Students could then do this as a writing activity or orally in pairs. Write new words on the board in sentences. **Omit if lack of time.**

Conclusion (5 minutes)

Activity E Students work in pairs. Check answers orally. **Omit if lack of time.**

Homework

Students write a description of the pictures.

Key

D 1 *Open answer*
   2 *Possible answer:*
      There's a woman and a baby in both pictures.
      There's a man in both pictures. He's looking at the woman and baby.
   3 *Possible answer:*
      Picture 1 shows a boat.
      Picture 2 shows fields and a tree.
      Picture 1 shows a happy woman.
      Picture 2 shows an unhappy woman.

E Countryside things and people: peasant, field, tree, village, gypsy
   Body and clothes: hips, bare feet, earrings, back, shoulder

3 Photographs (continued)

C Look at this picture. Then look at the two descriptions below. Which one describes the picture best?

1. *This picture shows countryside somewhere in Europe. A woman is sitting under a tree with her three children. The children's feet are bare. The children look poor and unhappy. Perhaps they're a gypsy family. I don't think the man is the woman's husband. I think he's just passing.*

2. *A woman with three small children is sitting under a tree in the middle of the countryside. The father is looking at his wife and children. The family is very poor – we can see this from their clothes. The baby is asleep under a tree. There's a village and fields in the background. Perhaps they're peasants – or gypsies. I'm not sure.*

D Answer these questions.

1. Which picture do you like best? Can you say why?

2. How are the two pictures similar? Use this language:
   There's/There are ... in both pictures.

3. How are they different? Use this language:
   The first picture shows ...
   The second picture shows ...

E Work in pairs. Put the following words into the two groups below:

hips peasant field bare feet earrings tree village back gypsy shoulder

Countryside things and people	Body and clothes

From *Instant Lessons 1 Elementary* edited by Peter Watcyn-Jones © Penguin Books 2000

Teacher's notes

4 I didn't do it!

Aim	To understand a jigsaw reading text.
Preparation	Copy the handouts on pages 19 and 21 – one copy per student. If required, cut text in Activity A into four sections.

Introduction *(5 minutes)*

Write these words on the board:
Today is a terrible day for me.
Ask:
Why do you think it is a terrible day for this person?
Elicit students' suggestions.

Presentation *(20 minutes)*

Activity A Students have to put sections a, b, c, d, into the right order to tell a story. You can do the activity in this way:
Students work in groups of four. Cut the story in Activity A into four sections, a, b, c, d. Give each member of a group one of the four sections. Each student reads his/her section. S/he must not show it to the other students. Then, as a group, students have to put the story together. They do this by telling each other about their section. They can read it to the rest of the group if they wish. Students use their dictionaries but don't try to understand every word. Alternatively, students can do the activity in pairs. In this case, give one student sections a and d. Give the other student sections b and c. If you don't wish to cut the story up, students can simply look at Activity A and do it from the page, but the group activity is probably the most useful, as students have to communicate with each other. Check answers orally, asking students to explain how they got to the answer. (In each text we are told the number of years the writer has been in prison.) Try not to elicit a lot of detail from students as the following activities deal with this.

The correct order is: c, b, d, a. When the story begins (text c), the writer (Peter) has been in prison for five years. This is because, when Peter's father died (more than five years ago), he (the father) gave all his money to Peter's brother John. John was murdered and the police thought Peter killed him because he wanted the money. So Peter was put in prison. However, his sister always believed in Peter (text b). In text d we learn that a dying man, Mike Rippon, has confessed to killing John. In text a, Peter is released from prison.

Practice *(25 minutes)*

Activities B and C In pairs, students read the texts in the correct order and answer the questions. Check answers orally, explaining where necessary.

(continued on page 20)

Key

A The correct order is: c, b, d, a
B 1 Peter
   2 He is in prison.
   3 He is at his sister's home.
   4 He is inside.
   5 Angry but happy to be out. Strange.
C 1e 2b 3d 4c 5a

(continued on page 20)

4 I didn't do it!

A Put the text in the right order.

a

Today I walked out of those doors into the sunlight. There were a lot of journalists. 'How do you feel?' they asked.

'Angry about those six and a half years. But happy to be out,' I answered. My sister was there. She took me back to her home and gave me a good meal.

All my old friends came. Some were very sorry. 'We thought you did it. We were wrong, Peter,' they said. But others said, 'We always believed in you.'

It is strange to be here, and look out onto a beautiful garden again. I can walk out into it if I want. I'm free.

b

Six years now. My sister came to see me this morning. She has been so good to me. She doesn't believe I killed John. 'I know you,' she said. 'You loved John. He was your brother! You didn't kill him! You didn't want his money.'

'I did,' I said. 'I wanted his money. When dad died and gave all his money to John, I was really angry! But kill my brother? No.'

She left and they took me outside for some exercise. One of the others came to talk to me.

'You know,' he said, 'I killed a man. But I'm beginning to believe you. I don't think you did.'

c

Today is a terrible day for me. They brought me here for the first time exactly five years ago. I remember it so well. The door closed behind me. They took my clothes, my money. They took my name and gave me a number. 'I didn't do it!' I told them. 'I didn't kill him!' They laughed and locked the door. The men inside laughed too. 'We all say that,' they said. 'No one's done anything wrong in here!'

d

I can't believe it! But it's true! They've found my brother's killer! His name is Mike Rippon. He's told the police he killed my brother all those years ago! My lawyer came to see me again this afternoon. 'Why did Rippon tell them?' I asked. 'It's more than six years now.'

'Rippon's very ill,' my lawyer answered. 'He's dying. He knows another man is in prison because of him. He wants to die a good man.' Soon I will be free.

B Work in pairs. Answer these questions.

1. What is the writer's name?
2. Where is the writer in texts b, c, and d?
3. Where is the writer in text a?
4. Is the writer inside or outside at the end of the story?
5. How does the writer feel when he is free?

C Work in pairs. Match the people (1–5) with the sentences (a–e).

1. John
2. the writer's lawyer
3. the writer's sister
4. Peter
5. Mike Rippon

a. This person is dying.
b. This person told the writer about Mike Rippon.
c. This person was in prison for six and a half years.
d. This person took Peter home and gave him a good meal.
e. This person was Peter's brother.

From *Instant Lessons 1 Elementary* edited by Peter Watcyn-Jones © Penguin Books 2000

Teacher's notes

Activities D and E Students work in pairs. Check answers orally, explaining where necessary.

Omit Activities C, D and E if lack of time. Instead, simply elicit the story from students. Write new words up on the board.

Activity F In pairs, students complete the sentences, then choose one of the conversations and act it out. Listen to some students and correct major errors.

Conclusion *(5 minutes)*

In one or two sentences, students explain orally why Peter was in prison. **Omit if lack of time.**

Homework

Students can do the conclusion activity as a written homework. They could also do any other omitted activities.

Key

D 1 The police believed the writer killed *John*.
   2 When he died, Peter's father gave all his money to *John*.
   3 The police believed Peter killed his *brother* because he wanted *his* money.
   4 Mike Rippon told *the police* that he killed John.
   5 Peter's sister *did not believe* that Peter was a killer.
   6 Peter was in prison for *six and a half* years.

E 1 a lawyer
   2 the police
   3 a journalist
   4 a prisoner

F a 1 brother   2 kill   3 money   4 wanted   5 died   6 angry   7 go/leave
   b 1 tell   2 years   3 dying   4 prison   5 man   6 free

4 I didn't do it! (continued)

D Work in pairs. Correct the mistakes in these sentences.
1. The police believed the writer killed Mike Rippon.
2. When he died, Peter's father gave all his money to Peter.
3. The police believed Peter killed his sister because he wanted her money.
4. Mike Rippon told Peter that he killed John.
5. Peter's sister believed that Peter was a killer.
6. Peter was in prison for five years.

E Work in pairs. Match the words with the sentences.

a prisoner   a journalist   the police   a lawyer

1. If the police think you killed someone, this person can help you.
2. These people try to find killers and put them in prison.
3. This person writes for newspapers.
4. This person is not free.

F Work in pairs. Complete these conversations. Try not to look at the text. Then look at the text and check your answers. Then choose one conversation and act it out.

a *Peter's sister:* I know you. You loved John. He was your (1)_____. You didn't (2)_____ him. You didn't want his (3)_____.

Peter: I did. I (4)_____ his money. When dad (5)_____ and gave all his money to John, I was really (6)_____. But kill my brother? No.

Peter's sister: I know that. Well, I must (7)_____ now. I'll come again soon.

b *Peter:* Why did Rippon (1)_____ them? It's more than six (2)_____ now.

Lawyer: Rippon's very ill. He's (3)_____. He knows another man is in (4)_____ because of him. He wants to die a good (5)_____.

Peter: So when will I be (6)_____?

Lawyer: Very soon.

From *Instant Lessons 1 Elementary* edited by Peter Watcyn-Jones © Penguin Books 2000

Teacher's notes

5 Health

Aim	To read about two people's lifestyles and assess how healthy they are.
Preparation	Copy the handouts on pages 23 and 25 – one copy per student.

Introduction *(5 minutes)*

Elicit/pre-teach the words *healthy* and *unhealthy*. Ask students: *Do you eat healthy food? If not, why not?* Elicit answers from students. A student may answer: *I eat too much butter and cheese.* Use the opportunity to elicit/teach the word *fat*, as in *Butter and oil are fats*.

Presentation *(20 minutes)*

Activity A In pairs, students read the health quiz, using their dictionaries where necessary. They discuss the questions and put a tick or cross beside each sentence.
Check answers orally, encouraging discussion. Correct major errors. Example language: *Red wine is good for you. Too much fat is bad for you.* Point out the uncountable nouns: *sugar/fruit/meat/honey is...* Write new words on the board in sentences.

Activity B In pairs, students answer the questions. Check answers orally, explaining where necessary. For question 4, encourage discussion. Example: *I eat a lot of fat. I don't eat enough vegetables.*

(continued on page 24)

Key

A 1 Right. Regular exercise stimulates the release of certain hormones/chemicals in the blood that make you feel good.
   2 Wrong, but you must eat carefully to make sure that you get enough vitamins and protein.
   3 Wrong. Both are carbohydrates that act very quickly to give you energy.
   4 Right. Otherwise, your metabolism is slow all day.
   5 Right. You must eat some fat in order to be healthy. Very little fat or no fat is bad for you.
   6 Wrong. Fat is worse for you than sugar. Too much fat can thicken your arteries so that the blood cannot get through.
   7 Wrong. People put on weight as they get older because they don't take much exercise.
   8 Wrong. You should eat five portions a day if you want to be really healthy and prevent dangerous illnesses.
   9 Wrong. Red wine is better for your heart than white wine.
  10 Wrong. Cooked tomatoes are better for you, as they protect you against certain kinds of cancer.

B 1 You feel very unhappy.
   2 a unhealthy   b uncooked   c worse
      d put on weight   e ill
   3 *Possible answer:* butter, oil, meat fat
   4 *Open answer*

(continued on page 24)

5 Health

A Work in pairs. Read through the Health Quiz. Do you think the sentences are right or wrong? Put a tick (✔) or cross (✘) next to each sentence. Then discuss your answers with the class.

Health Quiz

1 If you are depressed, exercise can help.

2 If you don't eat meat, you can get ill.

3 Honey is better for you than sugar.

4 You should always eat breakfast.

5 It is unhealthy to eat no fat.

6 Sugar is worse for you than fat.

7 People put on weight as they get older because their bodies slow down.

8 You should eat three portions of fruit and vegetables every day.

9 White wine is better for you than red wine.

10 Uncooked tomatoes are better for you than cooked tomatoes.

B Work in pairs. Answer these questions.

1 If you are depressed, how do you feel?

2 What is the opposite of these words?

   a healthy
   b cooked
   c better
   d lose weight
   e well

3 Name two fats.

4 Do you eat healthily or unhealthily? Say why.

From *Instant Lessons 1 Elementary* edited by Peter Watcyn-Jones © Penguin Books 2000

Teacher's notes

Practice *(20 minutes)*

Activity C Pre-teach the word *lifestyle*. In pairs, students read the two texts and complete the chart. They use dictionaries where necessary. Check answers orally, explaining where necessary. Correct major errors.

Activity D In pairs, students read the questions. Check understanding. Students discuss the questions in pairs. Then check answers orally, encouraging discussion for questions 3 and 4. You could then ask students to write their answers. Write new words on the board in sentences.

Conclusion *(5 minutes)*

Activity E Elicit a few sentences from students, for example: *You shouldn't smoke. You should eat more vegetables.* Students then write. Walk round and check their sentences.

Homework

Activity F Students write a short paragraph about their own lifestyle, using the texts in Activity C as a model.

Key

C

	Leo	Tania
Eats breakfast	✗	✔
Smokes	✗	✔
Eats a lot of fat	✔	✗
Eats meat	✔	✗
Drinks a lot of alcohol	✔	✗
Has a lot of friends	✔	✗
Eats a lot of fruit and vegetables	✗	✔
Exercises	✔	✔

D 1 *Possible answer:* He wakes with a headache because he drinks too much.
2 *Possible answer:* I think Tania wakes with a headache because she is lonely and unhappy.
3 *Possible answer:* Tania – she eats very little fat and doesn't drink.
4 *Possible answer:* Probaby Leo because he doesn't smoke.
5 *Possible answer:* No, a lot of people live like them. A lot of young women eat very little.
6 Open answer

F *Possible answer:*
Leo: You should eat more fruit and vegetables. You shouldn't drink so much.
Tania: You shouldn't smoke. You should talk to someone about your problems.

5 Health *(continued)*

C Read about the lifestyle of Leo and Tania. Then complete the chart below.

> Leo gets up at 7.45. He washes, throws on his clothes and drives to work. There he has a cup of black coffee with three teaspoons of sugar. At 10.30 he eats some chocolate and biscuits. For lunch he has a beer, two sandwiches, chips and an apple. After work he exercises for half an hour at the gym. He has a lot of friends and a very busy social life. After work, he sees his friends or girlfriend. He has a good meal in the evening – meat with vegetables, and dessert. He drinks a lot of beer each evening. He doesn't smoke. In the morning he often wakes up with a headache.

> Tania gets up at 7 o'clock every day. She has a cigarette before she gets up. For breakfast she eats toast and cottage cheese with no butter. She drinks two glasses of orange juice. She cycles to work and has some fruit at about eleven. For lunch she has a salad and some more fruit. After work she goes home and has a fish or vegetable main meal and a fruit salad. She doesn't eat meat or drink alcohol. She doesn't have many friends and often stays in. She's rather lonely. She smokes about twenty-five cigarettes a day. She often wakes up with a headache in the morning.

	Leo	**Tania**
Eats breakfast	✗	
Smokes		
Eats a lot of fat		
Eats meat		
Drinks a lot of alcohol		
Has a lot of friends		
Eats a lot of fruit and vegetables		✓
Exercises		

✓ = Yes   ✗ = No

D Work in pairs. Answer these questions.
1. Why do you think Leo wakes up with a headache in the morning?
2. Why do you think Tania wakes up with a headache?
3. Who do you think is thinner, Leo or Tania? Why?
4. Who do you think will live longer, Leo or Tania? Why?
5. Do you think the lifestyles of Leo and Tania are very unusual?
6. How do you feel when you read about Leo and Tania?

E You are a friend of Leo and Tania. Write your advice to one of them.
You should ...   *You shouldn't ...*

F Write four sentences about your lifestyle.

From *Instant Lessons 1 Elementary* edited by Peter Watcyn-Jones © Penguin Books 2000

Teacher's notes

6 The lottery ticket

Aim	To read a story and predict its ending.
Preparation	Copy the handouts on pages 27 and 29 – one copy per student.

Introduction *(5 minutes)*

Introduce the topic by asking student if they know these words: *lottery, lottery ticket, millionaire*. Write the words on the board. Ask students these questions: *How much can you win in a lottery? Can you become a millionaire? Do you buy lottery tickets? How often? Have you ever won anything?*

Presentation *(15–20 minutes)*

Activity A In pairs, students look at the pictures. Ask them what is happening in each picture. Before they read the text, ask students to order the pictures so that they make a story. Students then read the text and put the pictures in the right order. Encourage students to use their dictionaries. Check answers orally, explaining where necessary. Write new words on the board in sentences.

(continued on page 28)

Key

A Pictures d, e, c, a, b

(continued on page 28)

26

6 The lottery ticket

A Work in pairs. Put these pictures in order so they tell a story.

a

c

b

d

e

On Wednesday afternoon, Nick Bulmer spent £1 on a lottery ticket as usual. On Thursday afternoon, he returned from the car factory where he worked. He sat down to read the evening paper. Then he checked the winning lottery numbers. He couldn't believe his eyes!

'I've won!' he cried. 'I'm a millionaire! I must ring the lottery people and tell them!'

His phone wasn't working – he hadn't paid the bill – but there was a phone box at the end of the road. He put the ticket in his trouser pocket and ran out of the house. But because he was so excited, he didn't look where he was going and a car knocked him over. When Nick next woke up, he was in hospital with a big bandage on his head. His wife, Helen, was sitting next to him.

'What day is it?' he asked.

'Friday,' she said. 'You're lucky to be alive, Nick!'

'Where are my trousers?' said Nick anxiously.

'I took them home last night. They were covered in blood. I put them in the bin.'

'What?' shouted Nick, and told Helen about the lottery ticket.

'Oh no!' cried Helen. 'The dustmen are coming this morning.' And without another word she ran out of the room.

Now put the pictures in the order of the story.

From *Instant Lessons 1 Elementary* edited by Peter Watcyn-Jones © Penguin Books 2000

Teacher's notes

Practice *(20 minutes)*

Activity B In pairs, students answer the questions. Question 1: Use the questions to elicit the main points of the story from students. Question 3: Ask students to explain why Nick probably won't do a or c. Check answers orally, explaining where necessary. **Omit questions 3 and 4 if lack of time.**

Activity C In pairs, students read the two texts and say which one they prefer. Encourage students to use their dictionaries. Encourage discussion about the endings. Ask: *Why do you prefer ending 1?* Check the meaning of these words: *beach, quarrel, separate, search*. Correct major errors. If time, students can vote for the ending they prefer. Write new words on the board in sentences.

Optional Extension Students narrate the story from Nick's point of view (to a friend) as he waits for Helen's phone call.

Conclusion *(5–10 minutes)*

Activity D Elicit/teach the word *moral* (= the lesson of the story, what you can learn from the story). Students could have a brief discussion about the moral of each ending.

Homework

Students have to write seven sentences, each one including a word or phrase from Activity B, question 2.

Key

B 1 a She went home to look through the rubbish bags. She knew Nick's trousers were in one of them and the lottery ticket was in a trouser pocket.
    b Because she knew the dustmen were coming that morning.
    c Because he was in hospital with a big bandage on his head.
    d Perhaps because they didn't know their neighbours very well, or because they thought the neighbours might find the lottery ticket and keep it for themselves.

2 a car factory
   b He couldn't believe his eyes!
   c His phone wasn't working.
   d A car knocked him over.
   e You're lucky to be alive.
   f anxiously
   g I put them in the bin.

3 b Because if Helen doesn't find the trousers they will lose the ticket and the money.

4 *Open answer*

D *Possible answers:*
Always look where you're going. Don't run when you're excited. You can be happy without a lot of money. Money doesn't make you happy.

6 The lottery ticket *(continued)*

B 1 Answer these questions.

   a Where do you think Helen went? Why?

   b Why did she run?

   c Why couldn't Nick go?

   d Why do you think they didn't ring a neighbour and ask for help?

2 Which words in the text mean the same as these words?

   a A place where they make cars.

   b 'It can't be true!' he thought.

   c His telephone was out of order.

   d He had a car accident.

   e You nearly died.

   f In a worried voice.

   g I threw them away.

3 Which of these things do you think Nick will do while he waits to hear the answer from his wife? Say why you think this.

   a Pull the bedclothes over him and go to sleep.

   b Worry.

   c Laugh and say, 'What a joke!'

4 Translate these words into your own language.

   car factory   phone box

   bandage   dustmen

   anxious   bin

C Read these two endings to the story. Which one do you like best? Say why.

1 When Helen got back home, the dustmen were carrying bags of rubbish from the house.
   'Stop! Stop!' she cried. She took a rubbish bag and emptied it onto the ground. The trousers fell out, covered in blood. Helen put her hands in the pockets – and pulled out the lottery ticket.
   'Thank God!' she cried.
   A week later Nick and Helen were on a beach in Thailand. But they quarrelled about the money and six months later they separated.

2 Helen ran out of the hospital and jumped into her car. She drove fast and rather dangerously back home. Ten minutes later she was searching her dustbins. But the rubbish bags were gone.
   'Oh no!' she cried. 'It's not possible!'
   But it was. Nick and his wife never found their lottery ticket. And Nick still works in a car factory. But they are happy together and have two lovely children.

D Choose the ending you like best. What is the moral of the story? What lesson can you learn from it? Write one or two sentences.

From *Instant Lessons 1 Elementary* edited by Peter Watcyn-Jones © Penguin Books 2000

Teacher's notes

7 How do you sleep?

Aim	To do a questionnaire about sleeping habits and match problems with advice.
Preparation	Copy the handout on page 31 – one copy per student.

Introduction (5–10 minutes)

Ask students these questions. Elicit/teach the word *snore*.
Do you sleep well or badly? Do you snore?
Are you a 'morning' person or a 'night' person?
Then write the questions on the board. In pairs, students ask each other the questions.

Presentation (15 minutes)

Activity A Go through question 1 orally, asking individual students for their answers. Then students work through the quiz in pairs, ticking the answers that are truest for them. Tell them they must choose one answer only. Encourage them to use their dictionaries. Then go through the quiz orally, asking students for their answers. Explain anything important that they don't understand. Ask check questions, for example: *Why do you hate getting up?* Write new words on the board in sentences.

Optional Extension 1 Ask students to find someone in the class with five answers that are the same as theirs. Encourage them to say, for example:
We have the same/different answers for question 6.
We have four answers that are the same.

Optional Extension 2 In pairs, students discuss their sleeping habits with each other. (Hopefully, no misunderstandings here!)

Practice (20 minutes)

Activity B Again, encourage students to use their dictionaries. Then check answers orally, explaining where necessary.

Optional Extension Ask more questions about the words, for example: *How many pillows do you have? Do you ever use a hot water bottle?*

Activity C Go through the first two sentences orally. Ask students if they think this is good advice. Students do the rest in pairs, using their dictionaries. Then check answers orally. Explain anything important students don't understand. Ask students:
Do you agree with this advice? Why/Why not? How do you get to sleep?
Write new words on the board in sentences.

Conclusion (10 minutes)

In pairs, students read the text in Activity A again. Ask them: *Which sentences are real problems for someone?* Ask students to look through the advice in Activity C again and match the advice with the problem. For example, for 5c, number 2 is good advice.

Optional Extension Pairwork: Student A plays someone who can't sleep. He tells Student B his problems. Student B gives advice. Encourage students to use the imperative: *Have a routine. Wear thick socks.*

Homework

Students have to write down five more pieces of advice for someone who can't sleep, using the imperative.

Key

B 1 pillow
   2 nap
   3 hot water bottle
   4 snores
   5 dreamt

C *Possible answer:*
   1, 4, 5, 6, 7, 8

30

7 How do you sleep?

A Work in pairs. For each question, choose the answer that is true for you.

Quiz

1. a I go to sleep as soon as my head touches the pillow.
   b I take about an hour to go to sleep.
   c It takes me two to four hours to go to sleep.

2. a I need six hours' sleep or less each night.
   b I need seven to nine hours' sleep each night.
   c I need ten hours' sleep each night.

3. a I always feel I have had enough sleep.
   b I sometimes feel I have not had enough sleep.
   c I often feel tired during the day.

4. a I never wake during the night.
   b I wake once or twice during the night.
   c I often wake and can't get to sleep again.

5. a I get out of bed as soon as I wake up.
   b After I wake, it's about ten minutes before I get out of bed.
   c I hate getting up in the morning.

6. a I'm a 'morning' person. I go to bed early and I get up early.
   b I'm a 'night' person. I go to bed late and I get up late.
   c I go to bed at about eleven and get up at half past seven.

7. a I dream a lot and usually remember my dreams.
   b I sometimes remember my dreams.
   c I don't remember my dreams – or perhaps I don't dream!

8. a People tell me I snore loudly.
   b I sometimes snore.
   c I am sure I never snore.

B Work in pairs. Complete the sentences. Use these words:

dreamt   pillow   snores   nap   hot water bottle

1. At night, I rest my head on a ………………… .
2. I'm going to have a ………………… for half an hour.
3. I put a ………………… next to my feet.
4. I don't sleep well because my wife ………………… .
5. Last night I ………………… I was a dog.

C Work in pairs. Tick the advice which will help someone sleep.

1. Put a hot water bottle next to your feet or wear thick socks in bed.
2. Have a cup of tea or coffee.
3. Do some hard exercise just before you go to bed.
4. Finish your evening meal at least two hours before you go to bed.
5. Get up at the same time every morning.
6. Watch TV in bed or read in bed.
7. As you lie in bed, listen to all the sounds you can hear.
8. Have a regular bedtime routine.
9. Have a nap during the day.

From *Instant Lessons 1 Elementary* edited by Peter Watcyn-Jones © Penguin Books 2000

Teacher's notes

8 Help!

Aim	To read a story and predict what happens next.
Preparation	Copy the handouts on pages 33 and 35 – one copy per student.

Introduction *(5 minutes)*

Ask the students: *When do you say 'Help'?* Elicit suggestions from them. Say: *We're going to read a story. It's called 'Help'. What do you think it is about?* Elicit suggestions.

Presentation *(20 minutes)*

Activity A In pairs, students read the conversation and answer the questions. They use dictionaries where necessary. Check answers orally, explaining where necessary. Note: 999 is the Emergency Service in Britain. When you ring it, an operator asks: *Fire, ambulance or police?* Explain this to students. Encourage discussion for questions 8 and 9. Correct major errors. Students will probably want to use the words *burglar* and *afraid* so teach them. (*Burglar* is also needed for Activity B.)

Activity B In pairs, students read the conversation using their dictionaries, then they answer the questions. Check answers orally, explaining where necessary. Students will need to use the word *perhaps* so teach it if necessary. Write new words on the board in sentences.

(continued on page 32)

Key

A 1 They're at home, in bed.
    2 It's night.
    3 Because she hears something/noises downstairs.
    4 He's going downstairs. He thinks there's someone/a burglar in the house.
    5 Because he thinks that this person is dangerous.
    6 Because she wants the police to come.
    7 She feels afraid/frightened.
    8 *Possible answer:* There's a burglar in the house.
    9 *Possible answer:* He'll go downstairs and find the burglar. Perhaps they will fight. Or perhaps the burglar will run away.

B 1 *Possible answer:* Sarah runs downstairs because she hears a loud bang. Perhaps the burglar has a gun and he has used it.
    2 *Possible answer:* Perhaps the police will come and kill the burglar.

(continued on page 34)

8 Help!

A Work in pairs. Read this then answer the questions.

Sarah: Tony, wake up!
Tony: What, what?
Sarah: Listen!
Tony: My God! There's someone downstairs! I'll go and see.
(He gets out of bed.)
Sarah: No, don't do that, it's too dangerous. I'll ring 999.
(She picks up the phone.)
Tony: You do that. I'm going downstairs.
(He picks up a heavy vase.)
Sarah: No! He could have a knife – or a gun!
(She speaks into the phone.) Hello, we need help quickly!
Tony: I'm going downstairs.
(He leaves the room.)

1. Where are Sarah and Tony?
2. Is it day or night?
3. Why does Sarah wake Tony up?
4. Where is Tony going? Why?
5. Why does Tony pick up a heavy vase?
6. Why does Sarah ring 999?
7. How do you think Sarah feels?
8. What do you think Sarah will say next?
9. What do you think Tony will do?

B Work in pairs. Read this. Then answer the questions.

Operator: Fire, ambulance or police?
Sarah: *(on phone)* Police, please. There's a burglar in the house!
Operator: Can I have your address, please?
Sarah: 29, Clarendon Road. Please come quickly!
Operator: A police car will be with you in five minutes.
(There is the sound of a loud bang downstairs.)
Sarah: Oh my God! Tony!
(She throws the phone down and runs downstairs.)

1. What do you think has happened? Why does Sarah run downstairs?
2. What do you think will happen next?

Teacher's notes

Practice (25 minutes)

Activity C In pairs, students read the text without using their dictionaries. They guess the meaning of the underlined words. Check answers orally, explaining where necessary. Encourage students to use the context to guess. Show students the meaning of the words through the use of gesture. Then they read the text with dictionaries and complete the sentences. Check answers orally, explaining where necessary.

Activity D Question 1: In pairs or small groups, students finish the story in one or two sentences. Walk round and check what students have written, correcting major errors. For question 2, encourage discussion.

Activity E Students read the text and write answers to the questions. They use their dictionaries where necessary. If necessary, explain that the Beatles were a very famous pop group in the 1960s. Walk round and check what students have written. Also, check answers orally. Correct major errors. Write new words on the board in sentences. **Omit if lack of time.**

Conclusion (5 minutes)

Activity F Walk round and listen to students.

Homework

Activity G Check answers orally in the next lesson, explaining where necessary.

Key

C *push:* to move someone away from you with your hands
   seize: to take something quickly
   stab: to put a knife in someone
   drop: to let something fall
   Possible answer:
   1 ... the burglar wants to steal things. He wants to put them in the suitcase.
   2 ... then the man can't hurt him.
   3 ... the man wants to kill Tony.
E 1 In the story in the activities, Sarah and Tony wake because they hear noises in the house. Harrison and his wife also wake because they hear noises. Harrison goes downstairs and finds a burglar. The same happens with Tony. Harrison's wife saves him. Sarah saves Tony.
   2 The burglar attacks Tony with a gun. The burglar attacks George Harrison with a knife. Harrison's wife hits the burglar with a heavy vase. Sarah uses a kitchen knife.
G 1 a flowers
      b clothes, shoes, books and other things for a holiday
   2 a When you are in danger, for example, when there is a burglar in the house.
      b When you are suddenly very ill.
   3 pushed, dropped, seized
   4 Because he wants to steal things from it.
   5 A gun. It can kill more people more easily.
   6 *Open answer*

8 Help! (continued)

C Work in pairs. Read this. Guess the meaning of the four words underlined (lines 4, 5 and 6). Then complete the sentences.

Sarah runs into the kitchen. There she sees Tony fighting with a man of about thirty. The man is wearing jeans and a black jacket. There is a big suitcase on the floor. He has a gun in his hand and Tony is trying to get the gun from him. As the two men fight, the burglar <u>pushes</u> Tony on to the floor. Sarah sees that in two or three seconds the burglar will use the gun on Tony. Sarah <u>seizes</u> a kitchen knife and <u>stabs</u> the man in his right arm. He <u>drops</u> the gun and Sarah seizes it.

1   There is a suitcase on the floor because ...

2   Tony is trying to get the gun from the man because ...

3   Sarah stabs the man because ...

D Work in pairs or small groups. Answer the questions.

1   What do you think will happen next? Write two or three sentences and finish the story.

2   Do you think this story could happen? Who do you think is braver, Sarah or Tony?

E Read this and answer the questions.

In fact, something like this happened in 1999 to George Harrison and his wife (Harrison was once one of the four members of the Beatles pop group). They were asleep when they woke and heard a noise. Harrison went downstairs and found a man in the living room. The man attacked him with a knife and almost killed him. But Harrison's wife hit the man with a heavy vase and saved her husband's life.

1   How is this story about Harrison the same as the story in Activities A, B and C?

2   How is the story different?

F Work in pairs. Act out the scene in Activity A without looking at it. Then look and see if you were right. Then act it out again.

G Work in pairs. Answer these questions.

1   What do you put in   **a** a vase   **b** a suitcase?

2   When do you call   **a** the police   **b** an ambulance?

3   Complete these sentences using these words: *seized   dropped   pushed*

The young man _____ the old man against the wall. The old man _____ his wallet and the young man _____ it.

4   Why does a burglar enter a house?

5   Which is more dangerous, a knife or a gun? Why?

6   What sounds can you hear at the moment?

From *Instant Lessons 1 Elementary* edited by Peter Watcyn-Jones © Penguin Books 2000

Teacher's notes

9 A new life

Aim	To read a series of personal letters and deduce information about the writers.
Preparation	Copy the handouts on pages 37 and 39 – one copy per student. If required, cut up the four letters in Activity A.

Introduction *(5 minutes)*

Point to the map in the book and ask the students: *Where's Ireland?* Also ask: *What are people who live in Ireland called?* (answer: *Irish*). Find out what they know about Ireland.

Presentation *(15 minutes)*

Activity A Reading text. In this activity, students have to put letters a, b, c and d into the right order. You can do the activity in this way:

Students work in groups of four. Cut out the four letters in Activity A. Give each member of a group one of the letters, a, b, c or d. Each student reads his/her letter. S/he must not show it to the other students. Then, as a group, students have to put the story together. They do this by telling each other about their letter. They can read it to the rest of the group if they wish. Students use their dictionaries but don't try to understand every word.

Alternatively, students can do the activity in pairs. In this case, give one student letters a and b. Give the other student letters c and d. If you don't wish to cut the story up, students can simply look at Activity A and do it from the page, but the group activity is probably more useful, as students have to communicate with each other. Check answers orally, asking students to explain how they got to the answer. Try not to elicit a lot of detail from students as the following activities deal with this.
(The correct order is: c, a, d, b. The situation is that an Irishman and his wife, Patrick and Marie, have emigrated to New York. They have been there for a month when Patrick writes his first letter to his brother Paul in Ireland.)

(continued on page 38)

Key

A *The order is:* c, a, d, b

(continued on page 38)

9 A new life

Where's Ireland?

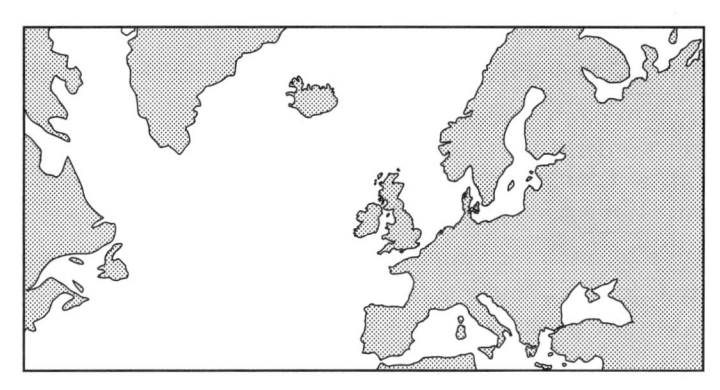

A Work in pairs or groups of four. Read these letters and put them in the right order.

a

Dear Patrick,
I was so pleased to get your letter. We talk about you and Marie all the time. We miss you. Here in Dublin it's rained for a month without stopping. Does it rain like that in New York? Tell me, I need to know. If it does, I'm not going to come and join you. If it doesn't, then I can sleep on your floor when I arrive. I mean it. But it's true, I miss my elder brother and his pretty wife. But in your next letter, Patrick, tell us more about the place. What are the women like? Do they all smoke?
Write soon.
Love, Paul

b

Dear Patrick,
I bought my ticket yesterday. It was expensive, but Father helped me.
'Do you want me to leave you and Mother, then?' I asked.
'Yes, because in another year, I'm coming too. I want a good home ready for me,' he answered.
He means it, you know. We'll all be over there soon.
Patrick, will you meet me when I arrive? I'm sailing on the Good Hope. It arrives on Wednesday, July 25th at four in the afternoon. Stay well and love to Marie.
Love, Paul

c

Dear Paul,
We've been here a month now, Marie and I. When I open my eyes in the morning, I can't believe I'm here. When we arrived, Marie's cousins took us to their home. We stayed there for two weeks but now we have a small place of our own. They're poor, her cousins. America hasn't made them rich. But they were kind to us and looked after us well.
'Will you return to Ireland?' I asked them. 'Never,' they said. 'It's better to be poor here than in Ireland. People are kinder. I've found work in a factory. Marie cleans the house of a rich Irish woman twice a week. It's a beginning. Perhaps one day we'll have a cleaner!
Write to me, Paul.
Love, Patrick

d

Dear Paul
Yes, the women all smoke. Everyone smokes in America. It's a crazy place. When I walk in the streets, I see people from all over the world - Chinese, Italian, Irish, German... You go to one part of New York and you think you're in China. You go to another part and everyone is speaking Italian. And me, I live in the Irish part of New York - it's called the Bronx. I could live here all my life and only speak to Irishmen, you know.
We are doing all right, Marie and I. Working hard, but we are not hungry, and once a month we eat in a restaurant, Paul! When are you going to come and join us?
Love, Patrick

From *Instant Lessons 1 Elementary* edited by Peter Watcyn-Jones © Penguin Books 2000

Teacher's notes

Practice *(25 minutes)*

Activity B In pairs, students read the letters in the correct order. They answer the questions. Check answers orally, explaining where necessary. Write new words on the board in sentences.

Activity C In pairs, students correct the mistakes in the sentences. Check answers orally.

Activity D In pairs, students write answers to these questions. Walk round and check what students have written. Also check answers orally. Write model answers on the board.

Activity E Students do this in pairs. You may want to begin by eliciting ideas for the letter from students and writing the ideas on the board. Walk round and check what students have written. **If lack of time, omit and do for homework.**

Conclusion *(5 minutes)*

Activity F Students discuss in pairs. Then have a brief class discussion. Put some example sentences on the board.

Homework

Students write a short answer to Activity F. Walk round and check their answers in the next class.

Key

B 1 1903. Many Irish people went to America around this time. Also, we know that Paul is going to take a boat to America. In 1983, people almost always flew. In 1783, the arrival time of a boat would not be very accurate because it depended on the wind, but Paul says he will be arriving at 4pm.
 2 Because they were poor in Ireland. They hope they can have a better life in America.
 3 a They are kind to Patrick and his wife. When Patrick and Marie arrive in New York their cousins take them to their home. Patrick and Marie stay there for two weeks. Patrick's cousins are poor, but they are happier than they were in Ireland.
  b Patrick's brother is called Paul. He is younger than Patrick. He wants to go to America too. He doesn't like Ireland – it rains too much. He lives in Dublin. In his last letter, he says that he is sailing to America and will arrive on July 25th.
  c They want to go to America too. They give money to Paul for the boat journey.
  d Her name is Marie and she is pretty. She finds work in New York as a cleaner for a rich Irish woman. She cleans her house twice a week.

C 1 Patrick is in <u>New York, America</u>.
 2 Patrick is <u>Irish</u>.
 3 Patrick has been in America for <u>one</u> month when he writes his first letter to Paul.
 4 Patrick finds a job in a <u>factory</u>.
 5 Dublin is in <u>Ireland</u>.
 6 Paul hates the rain in <u>Dublin</u>.
 7 There are <u>Chinese, Italians, Irish and Germans</u> in New York.
 8 Paul is <u>sailing</u> to New York.
 9 Paul is arriving at four in the <u>afternoon</u>.

D 1 When s/he is away from you and you love or like him/her very much.
 2 They do the same work all the time. In a factory, machines make things and people help the machines.
 3 *Possible answer:* It's warm and sunny.
 4 It's a ship/a big boat.
 5 About two weeks.
 6 No, they usually fly. They don't go by boat because it takes longer and is more expensive.

9 A new life (continued)

B Work in pairs. Read the letters again in the right order. Answer these questions.

1 When do you think Patrick and Paul wrote these letters? Why do you think this?

   a 1983   b 1903   c 1758

2 Why have Patrick and his wife gone to another country to live?

3 What do we learn about these people:

   a Marie's cousins   b Patrick's brother   c Patrick's parents   d Patrick's wife

C Work in pairs. Correct the mistakes in these sentences.

1 Patrick is in London, England.
2 Patrick is Italian.
3 Patrick has been in America for three months when he writes his first letter to Paul.
4 Patrick finds a job in a shop.
5 Dublin is in Italy.
6 Paul hates the rain in Italy.
7 There are only Englishmen in New York.
8 Paul is flying to New York.
9 Paul is arriving at four in the morning.

D Work in pairs. Write answers to these questions.

1 When do you miss someone?
2 What kind of work do people do in factories?
3 What's the weather like today?
4 Paul tells Patrick that he is sailing on the *Good Hope*. What is the *Good Hope*?
5 How long do you think the journey will take?
6 Do you think that people often sail to America today? If not, why not?

E Work in pairs. Imagine that Paul is with his brother in America. Write Paul's first letter to his father.

F Would you like to go and live in another country? Write one or two sentences about this.

From *Instant Lessons 1 Elementary* edited by Peter Watcyn-Jones © Penguin Books 2000

Teacher's notes

10 Postcards

Aim	To read a series of postcards and deduce the outcome of the holiday.
Preparation	Copy the handouts on pages 41 and 43 – one copy per student.

Introduction (5 minutes)

Ask students: *Which three places would you most like to go to in Europe? Why?* They can answer it in pairs. If the question is too difficult, they need not repeat it. Get some answers from students.

Presentation (15 minutes)

Activity A Ask: *What's a postcard?* Use the handout to show them. Students work in pairs, only using dictionaries if absolutely necessary. Check they understand the tasks before they read the postcards. Check answers orally, referring to the texts. Also, look at their maps. Elicit or explain meaning where necessary. Write new words on the board in sentences.

Practice (20 minutes)

Activity B Students work in pairs. Check they understand the questions. This time, students can use their dictionaries. Tell them not to try to understand every word. Check their answers orally, referring to the texts. Elicit or explain meaning where necessary. Question 4: Encourage students to talk here.

(continued on page 42)

Key

A 1/2 1 Rome 2 Barcelona 3 Paris
   3 Rome: 3 days   Barcelona: 2 days   Paris: 7 days
B 1 camera/Barcelona: Helen lost her camera in Barcelona.
      river/Paris: Helen fell into the river in Paris.
      jacket/Rome: Someone stole Helen's jacket in Rome.
   2 In London.
   3 a nightclubs, bars, discos, etc.
      b When you have seen Rome, you can die happy.
   4 *Possible answer:* Yes, I do. I like going to nightclubs, because I like dancing.
   5 Museums often have old things in them. Many of Rome's buildings are hundreds of years old. Also, Rome is full of statues and paintings.

(continued on page 42)

10 Postcards

A Work in pairs. Read these postcards. Two young women are travelling round Europe together.

1. Put 1, 2 and 3 on the map, for the first, second and third city they visit.
2. Draw a line to show Sandra and Helen's journey on the map.
3. Write in the number of days they stay.

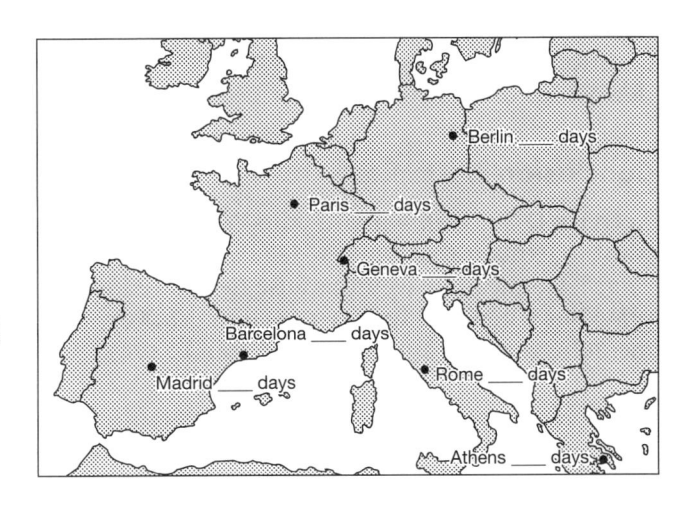

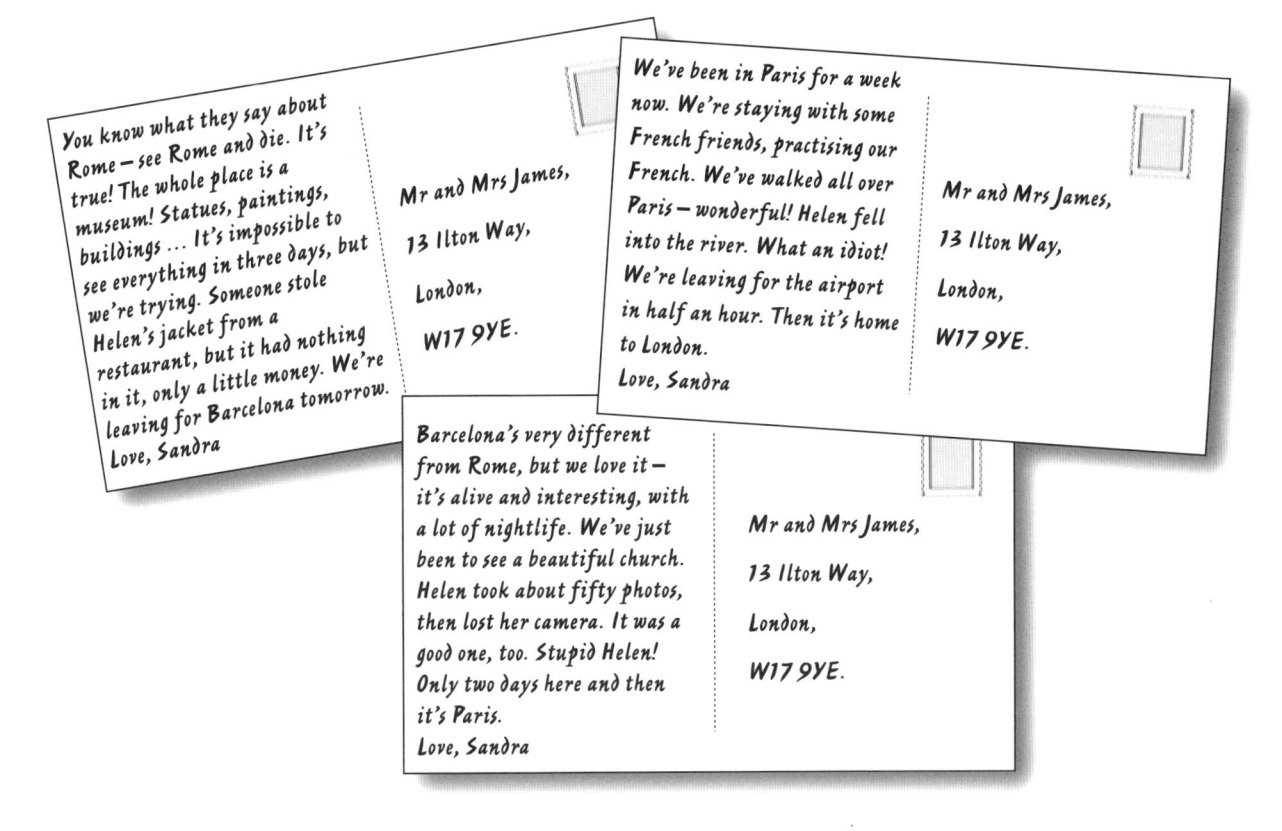

Map shows: Berlin ___ days, Paris ___ days, Geneva ___ days, Barcelona ___ days, Madrid ___ days, Rome ___ days, Athens ___ days.

Postcard 1:

You know what they say about Rome – see Rome and die. It's true! The whole place is a museum! Statues, paintings, buildings... It's impossible to see everything in three days, but we're trying. Someone stole Helen's jacket from a restaurant, but it had nothing in it, only a little money. We're leaving for Barcelona tomorrow.
Love, Sandra

Mr and Mrs James,
13 Ilton Way,
London,
W17 9YE.

Postcard 2:

We've been in Paris for a week now. We're staying with some French friends, practising our French. We've walked all over Paris – wonderful! Helen fell into the river. What an idiot! We're leaving for the airport in half an hour. Then it's home to London.
Love, Sandra

Mr and Mrs James,
13 Ilton Way,
London,
W17 9YE.

Postcard 3:

Barcelona's very different from Rome, but we love it – it's alive and interesting, with a lot of nightlife. We've just been to see a beautiful church. Helen took about fifty photos, then lost her camera. It was a good one, too. Stupid Helen! Only two days here and then it's Paris.
Love, Sandra

Mr and Mrs James,
13 Ilton Way,
London,
W17 9YE.

B Work in pairs. Read the postcards again. Answer these questions.

1. Draw lines between these words to show the connections. Then explain the connections.

   camera   Paris   jacket   river   Rome   Barcelona

2. Where are Sandra and Helen going to be in four hours?
3. Explain these phrases.
   a nightlife   b See Rome and die
4. Do you look for nightlife when you go on holiday? Why/why not?
5. Why does Sandra say Rome is a museum?

From *Instant Lessons 1 Elementary* edited by Peter Watcyn-Jones © Penguin Books 2000

Teacher's notes

Activity C Same steps as Activities A and B. For questions 6, encourage students to talk. Write new words on the board in sentences.

Conclusion (10 minutes)

Activity D Students work in pairs. You might want to explain that when we say *he went to church*, we mean he went because he wanted to pray; but when we say *he went to a church*, we mean he went for another reason (not to pray).

Activity E If you have time, when students have performed the task, elicit this kind of language: *I put 'art galleries' first because I love art ... I put 'nightlife' last because I don't like going to nightclubs.*

Homework

Students write Sandra's fifth postcard. Students must decide whether she has found a job or not.

Key

C 1 They are still in Paris because Helen fell down the stairs at the airport and hurt her back. Helen is in hospital.
 2 Because she thinks Helen has been very lucky. Helen has met a rich man and he wants to marry her.
 3 Yes. Bad things often happen to Helen – she has accidents. Perhaps she isn't very careful. Or perhaps she's always thinking about something else and doesn't notice things.
 4 Sandra thinks Helen is rather stupid. She says: 'Stupid Helen! She really is an idiot.' She's also jealous: 'Some people have all the luck.'
 5 No, she's going to stay in Paris and try to find a job. Perhaps this is because she wants to marry a rich businessman too.
 6 *Possible answer:* Yes, it's always nice to be rich./No, you can be happy without a lot of money.

D 1 *Possible answer:* I went to a museum last summer. I went to an art gallery last week. I went to church last Sunday. I went to an airport six months ago, when I went to France on holiday.
 2 *Open answer*

10 Postcards *(continued)*

C Work in pairs. Read the fourth postcard. Answer these questions.

> We're still in Paris! Helen fell down the stairs at the airport!! She hurt her back and is in hospital! She really is an idiot! But it's not serious – she'll be out tomorrow. A rich businessman took her to hospital. They're in love and he wants to marry her! Some people have all the luck! I've decided to stay and find a job. Perhaps I'll fall down some stairs too …
>
> Love Sandra
>
> Mr and Mrs James,
> 13 Ilton Way,
> London,
> W17 9YE.

1 Where are they? Why? What happened? Where's Helen?
2 Why does Sandra write: *Some people have all the luck*?
3 Is Helen unlucky?
4 How does Sandra feel about Helen?
5 Is Sandra going back to London? Why/why not?
6 Do you think Helen is 'lucky' to marry a rich businessman? Why/why not?

D Work in pairs. Answer these questions.

1 When did you last go to these places?

   a museum   an art gallery   a church   an airport

2 Name a famous example of these.

   a statue   a painting   a building

E Which of these things are important to you when you are on holiday in a foreign city? Put them in order 1–5. Then explain your reasons to another student.

nightlife   _____
museums   _____
art galleries   _____
good restaurants   _____
beautiful buildings _____

Is there anything else which is important to you?

From *Instant Lessons 1 Elementary* edited by Peter Watcyn-Jones © Penguin Books 2000

Writing: Lessons 11–20

11 Consequences

Aim	To work on a simple story collectively and then to write it up individually.
Preparation	Copy the handout on page 45 – one copy per student.

Introduction *(5 minutes)*

Introduce the idea of party games – maybe you went to a party recently and played some. Ask what games can be played with a piece of paper. Answers could include drawing things for others to guess, finding as many words as possible from one big word, etc.

Presentation *(10 minutes)*

Write the word *Consequences* on the board and explain that this is what happens as a result of something else. It is also a popular party game played with paper and pen. Give out the handouts and explain that each person writes something in a box, folds the paper over so that it cannot be seen and passes it on to the next person, who writes something in the next box, etc. Do one on the board as an example, asking students to suggest the names of a man and a woman for the first two boxes and a place and time for the next two. For example:
Arnold Schwarzenegger met the Queen of England in New York on Christmas Day. He said 'How are you?' She said 'I like your T-shirt.' The consequence was they went dancing together.

Practice 1 *(15 minutes)*

Students now play a game of Consequences. Everyone should fill in the first box, and then fold it over and pass it to their neighbour at exactly the same time. Give time for ideas and circulate to help with the writing of them. When the consequence (the final box) has been written, the paper is passed to the next person who opens the whole paper and reads it silently.

Practice 2 *(15 minutes)*

Each student now works individually to write out their story in full. They should keep to what has been said but should correct it if necessary and add a few details to the consequence. Suggest that anyone who finishes before the others can try to add a moral. *The moral of this story is ...*

Conclusion *(5 minutes)*

The finished stories can be read out to the class, either by the authors or by you, and a few favourites chosen.

Homework

Put a list of some interesting and unusual men and women (real and imaginary) on the board. Students choose two to meet and try to construct a possible meeting place, conversation and consequence.

11 Consequences

Fold

met

Fold

in

Fold

on

Fold

He said:

Fold

She said:

Fold

The consequence was:

Teacher's notes

12 Four easy steps

Aim	To learn how to write simple instructions for a range of activities, both everyday and imaginative.
Preparation	Copy and cut up the handout on page 47 – one per group of 2–4 students.

Introduction (5 minutes)

Come into the class yawning and say you have not been sleeping well and would like some advice on how to get a good night's sleep. Write on the board *How to get to sleep* and ask for suggestions. Write all these down and then say that you'll never remember all that ... so you write a second heading, *Four easy steps to getting to sleep*, and condense what was suggested, using *First ... / Then ... / Next ... / Finally, ...* to show the sequence. For example:
First have a warm bath. Then get into a comfortable bed. Next read an interesting book. Finally, turn out the light and close your eyes.

Presentation (20 minutes)

Divide the class into small groups (two to four students) and give each group the top four sets of easy steps, cut up into twenty pieces and all mixed up. The aim of the activity is to put together the four easy steps to do each activity. Students should be encouraged to find the four titles and then the first three steps that go with each one, using the markers *First ...*, *Then ...* and *Next ...*, and noting the appropriate vocabulary. Once this has been completed, students will see that the fourth easy step is indicated by the word *Finally ...* but has been left blank. They now work together in their groups to write a short and simple final instruction for each activity. Check the answers on the board and the class can choose the best one for each set. (Possible answers: *Finally, put the omelette on a plate and eat it. / Finally, when the person answers, say hello. / Finally, watch your programme and turn off when it's finished. / Finally, get into the shower and wash yourself.*)

Practice (25 minutes)

Tell the class that now that they know how to write instructions you are going to move on from everyday activities to things that are really worth knowing! Say that you would like to know how to win the lottery, become a film star, see a ghost, etc.
Ask the class what they would like to know how to do and write these on the board. Try to get a good selection. (Ideas could include: how to pass exams / how to have lots of friends / how to appear on television / how to become president / how to have nice dreams / how to be very fit / how to look smart / how to impress people / how to win at cards / how to avoid doing any washing up, etc.)
Students now go back into their groups to choose two of these activities (or make up two of their own) and work together to write four easy steps to achieving them. Distribute the remaining two tables on the handout for them to fill in and circulate to give help where necessary.

Conclusion (5 minutes)

When the groups are ready, a spokesperson reads out the four easy steps and the rest of the class tries to guess what these steps are leading to. Comment can also be elicited as to how useful they are!

Homework

Students can write up one or two of their favourite ideas and perhaps add: *Four easy steps to good English*.

12 Four easy steps

Four easy steps to making an omelette	Four easy steps to making a phone call
First buy some eggs.	First decide who to phone.
Then go into the kitchen.	Then pick up the receiver.
Next cook the eggs.	Next dial the number.
Finally,	Finally,

Four easy steps to watching television	Four easy steps to having a shower
First turn on the television.	First go into the bathroom.
Then choose an interesting programme.	Then get a towel and soap.
Next sit down in a comfortable chair.	Next turn on the water.
Finally,	Finally,

Four easy steps to	Four easy steps to ....
First	First
Then	Then
Next	Next
Finally,	Finally,

From *Instant Lessons 1 Elementary* edited by Peter Watcyn-Jones © Penguin Books 2000 — **Photocopiable**

Teacher's notes

13 World weather reports

Aim	To write a simple weather report giving temperature and general climactic conditions.
Preparation	Copy the handout on page 49 – one copy per student.
(Optional)	Bring in five large pieces of paper and five marker pens.

Introduction *(5 minutes)*

Make some remark about the weather (*It's very cold/hot today,* etc.) and ask students if they agree. Get them talking briefly about recent weather. Explain that in Britain the weather is a very popular topic and usually a good way to start a conversation. Write a few opening remarks on the board, for example: *What a cold day! Lovely weather today! What awful rain!* Ask students to turn to those beside them and open a conversation. Their partners can briefly respond with: *Yes, it is./Yes, I agree.*

Presentation *(15 minutes)*

Divide the class into two and ask one half to write down all the words they know for 'bad' weather and the other half to write down words for 'good' weather. Set a time limit of about 3 minutes. Then write the words up on the board in two columns. There may be some that appear in both lists and this could be a good starting point for a short discussion of what makes good or bad weather; for example: *Is rain good or bad?* Explain that they are going to write their own weather reports and that as an example you are going to read them a short weather report for South America. Read the following passage, giving students time to write:
The weather in South America today is generally sunny and hot. There is some rain in the north and snow in the south. It's windy in the north east. Now for some details: the average temperature in Rio de Janeiro is 29 degrees centigrade and in Lima it's 30 degrees. It's a good day to go to the beach.
Then distribute handouts and ask them to check that what they've written ties in with the details on the map and statistics at the top of the page. Check that everyone understands the report.

Practice *(25 minutes)*

Divide the class into five groups and give each group a continent to work on. They work together to write the weather report for their continent, incorporating the statistics on the handout and adding other information if they wish. If possible, give students a large piece of paper and a marker pen so that they can prepare a weather map with symbols and temperatures to illustrate what they say (as in a TV weather report) as they present it to the class.
Groups listen carefully to one another's reports and mark what is said each time on the relevant map on their own sheets. Comment on the clarity and accuracy of the presentations and ask students to compare their work with a neighbour's to see if they have understood the same thing each time.

Conclusion *(5 minutes)*

Write a few more unusual weather words on the board, and any that are particularly relevant to local conditions, for example: *monsoon, drought, hurricane, snowstorm, thunderstorm,* etc. Ask the class to suggest some symbols for them. Finally, ask: *How much are we influenced by the weather?*

Homework

Students could try their hand at weather forecasting by writing a forecast for the day they have their next English lesson. This could then be compared with the actual weather on that day.

13 World weather reports

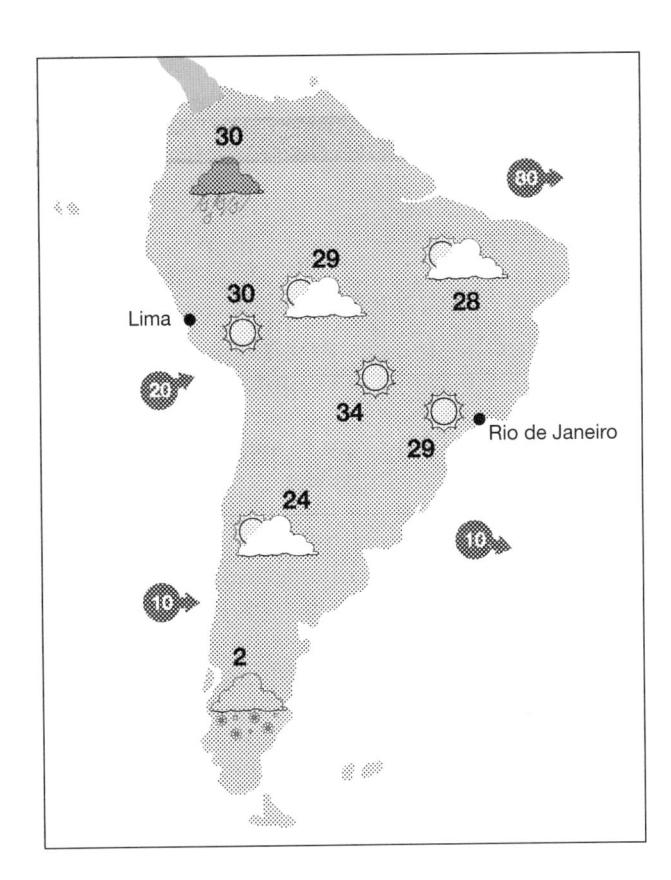

	°C	
Adelaide	30	Dry and sunny
Beijing	8	Dry and sunny
Cairo	20	Dry and sunny
Johannesburg	21	Bright and breezy
Lima	30	Dry and sunny
Madrid	13	Mostly dry and bright
Melbourne	18	Dry, rather cloudy
Montreal	−6	Snow showers
Nairobi	22	Rain early, sun later
New Delhi	23	Fair with some cloud
New York	6	Cool with showers
Paris	10	Dry with sunny spells
Rio de Janeiro	29	Dry and sunny
Rome	15	Cloudy with rain at times
Sydney	25	Dry and sunny
Tokyo	11	Cool and cloudy
Washington	5	Cool, showers later

From *Instant Lessons 1 Elementary* edited by Peter Watcyn-Jones © Penguin Books 2000

Teacher's notes

14 Food for thought

Aim	To practise writing simple shopping lists and menus.
Preparation	Copy the handout on page 51 – one copy per student.

Introduction *(5 minutes)*

Introduce the topic of food and drink by saying that you are hungry and by suggesting what you would like to eat. See if students agree with you. Divide the class into six groups and give each group a category: *vegetables, fruit, meat, dairy products, drinks, cereal-based products*. Give them 2 minutes to write down as many items as they can under their heading. Listen to all the groups and write any new vocabulary on the board. Point out that we list food when we make a shopping list.

Presentation *(20 minutes)*

Give each student a copy of the handout and explain that they are going to write a shopping list for themselves of all the things they would need if they invited a group of friends round for a birthday supper. First they will have to decide on the menu (suggest they keep this very simple) and second on the quantities. Using some of the items already mentioned, ask how they are bought, for example: *oranges – by the kilo*. Elicit the following words: *kilo, bottle, packet, can, loaf, carton*. Write these on the board.

They now work on their shopping lists in small groups (three to six students) and then present these to the class. Invite comment, both on the menu and on the quantities. What would be their ideal supper menu?

Practice *(20 minutes)*

Explain to the students that unfortunately the supper they planned is a disaster. Both gas and electricity workers are on strike, so they can't cook anything. Ask them to suggest what they can do instead, eliciting/teaching *take-away*. Draw their attention to the publicity flyer on the handout and explain that they have to choose one of the food categories listed and write the menu. First, elicit a couple of suggestions of food and drink to include on each menu and write them on the board. Then students work in groups of four to write one of the menus. Walk round the class, giving vocabulary and encouragement as required. For whole class feedback, the menus could be stuck up round the room and the students could circulate to choose their favourite. If there is time, you might like to discuss pricing and ideas of other food categories that could be bought as a take-away.

Conclusion *(5 minutes)*

Write on the board:
healthy   unhealthy
Say some food words and ask students to tell you if they are healthy or unhealthy. For example: *hamburgers, tomatoes, chips, salad, fish, chocolate, crisps, spinach*. Then look back at the food categories at the take-away restaurant. Are there some food categories which are usually more healthy than others?

Homework

To write a menu and shopping list for a lunch for six people.

50

14 Food for thought

Birthday Invitation

Please come to my birthday party on Saturday 18th November at 6 o'clock. We'll have dancing, supper and watch a video.

R.S.V.P.

Shopping List (for 10)

---

7 restaurants in 1 – in the comfort of your own home!

7 different take-away menus, each one with an expert chef to prepare your meal.

Choose from:
traditional, Italian, Mexican, Chinese, ice cream parlour, burger bar, salad bar.

MENU

To eat   *To drink*

Teacher's notes

15 My ideal penfriend

Aim	To write a simple letter about oneself and then to reply to a letter.
Preparation	Copy the handout on page 53 – one copy per student.
(Optional)	Bring in a letter you have received from another country.

Introduction *(5 minutes)*

Tell the class that you have just received an interesting letter from a foreign friend/penfriend (show a letter if you have one). Talk about the pleasure of receiving mail and explain about penfriends. Ask if anyone in the class has one and, if so, discuss briefly.

Presentation *(15 minutes)*

Explain that everyone is going to choose an ideal penfriend – someone they would be interested to write to and get a letter from. Stress that this can be anyone they choose. Ask for suggestions and make a list on the board. This could include famous sports people, film stars, historical figures, characters in books, beings from other planets, people from the future, animals, etc.
Give out the handout and draw attention to the layout of a letter, i.e. the position of the address, the date, the greeting (*Dear ...*), the paragraphs, the close. Read the first list. Divide the class into small groups and ask them to add details of what else they would say about themselves. Listen to suggestions and write some up on the board. Then look at the second list and ask them to go back in their groups to think of what else it would be interesting to know about a new penfriend. Discuss briefly.

Practice *(30 minutes)*

The students now work individually for about 10 minutes to write a short letter to their chosen penfriend. Circulate to give help and encouragement. Weaker students should be encouraged to write something simple and clear while the stronger students can be more adventurous. Make sure everyone addresses their letter clearly and also signs their name. Take in all the letters and then redistribute them. Students now have a new letter and their task is to write a short reply. Spend a few minutes discussing what might go into this letter, for example: thanks for the original letter, responding to some of the information given, answering the questions, asking some more questions, close, etc.
Give up to 10 minutes for the replies to be written. Then give the replies back to the original senders to read.

Conclusion *(5 minutes)*

Put students into small groups and ask them to read the letters and replies and choose one pair to read to the whole class. Listen and comment.
Optional Extension Talk about what makes a good letter.

Homework

Students could rewrite their letters using ideas from the classwork, aiming to make them as interesting as possible. This could even lead on to the class having real penfriends in an English-speaking country.

15 My ideal penfriend

About me:
what I look like – shall I send a photo?
family and friends
where I live
likes and dislikes
hopes and dreams – even the unrealistic ones!
And I mustn't forget ...

....
....
....
....
....

Things I want to know:
a typical day in my penfriend's life
favourite things: food, films, books, animals, etc.
childhood memories – good or bad?
plans for the future
... and of course ...

....
....
....
....
....

Teacher's notes

16 Advice from Anna

Aim	To be able to give simple written advice on a variety of topics using appropriate structures.
Preparation	Copy the handout on page 55 – one copy per four students and one extra. Cut the sheet up into the four letter sections.

Introduction (5 minutes)

Say you have a problem and ask the class to advise you; for example, you've left all your money at home / you've lost your door key / your shoe has a hole, etc. Ask who they go to when they need advice and introduce the idea of writing to a stranger in a magazine or newspaper. (You might like to write *agony aunt* on the board and explain it.)

Presentation (15 minutes)

Write the following on the board:
Dear Anna,
I am an English teacher and I have a very difficult class who don't like English. What can I do?
Invite the class to be Anna and give some advice. As they suggest things, list these on the board using a variety of advice structures, for example:
You should make your lessons more interesting.
Why don't you sing English songs?
If I were you, I'd ask the class why they don't like English.
You could teach Spanish instead!
Ask the head teacher to help you.
Good luck! etc.
Focus attention on the advice structures and how to use them.

Practice (25 minutes)

Give each student one of the problem letters. Working individually, they read about the problem and then write some advice underneath, using a variety of structures. Set a time limit and collect all the letters. Divide the class into four groups and redistribute the letters by problem, i.e. one group will receive all the letters about the man and his boss, etc. Members of each group work together to read all the different advice given for their particular problem and choose the best ideas. They then decide how best to express this and write a final short letter of advice incorporating the most sensible ideas.
Problems and solutions are read to the whole class and comment invited.

Conclusion (5 minutes)

Give the following advice and ask for suggestions as to what the problem could be (the funnier the better):
You should turn on the radio and dance!

Homework

To write a problem letter and give advice (based on a real or imagined problem).

16 Advice from Anna

your problems ...

Q *Dear Anna,*
Every day when I go to work I see the same girl on the bus and I would like to get to know her. What should I do?

Paul

A

your problems ...

Q *Dear Anna,*
At school everyone laughs at me because I am so tall and I have no friends. What can I do?

Julia

A

your problems ...

Q *Dear Anna,*
My boyfriend is a student and has no money so I always have to pay for everything. It's very expensive. What should I do?

Maria

A

your problems ...

Q *Dear Anna,*
My boss often makes mistakes and this causes problems at work. He's the boss so it's difficult for me to say anything. What can I do?

David

A

From *Instant Lessons 1 Elementary* edited by Peter Watcyn-Jones © Penguin Books 2000 — Photocopiable

Teacher's notes

17 Colours

Aim	To write a simple story, incorporating words previously worked on, and to compare stories.
Preparation	Copy the handout on page 57 – one copy per student.
(Optional)	Bring in some brightly coloured objects to introduce the topic.

Introduction *(5 minutes)*

Revise the English words for the different colours by showing the objects you have brought in or by talking about objects in the classroom. Tell the students your favourite colour and invite them to tell you theirs. You might like to see which colour is the class favourite.

Presentation *(10 minutes)*

Give out the handouts and divide the class into four groups. Each group has a colour (red, white, blue or green) and they have 3 minutes, working individually and together, to write down as many words in English connected with that colour as they can (for *red*, for example: *angry, tomato ...*)
Then write all the words on the board, explaining where necessary and encouraging the class to note these down in the appropriate boxes on their handouts.

Practice *(30 minutes)*

Each person now chooses three of the words from their colour list and draws or writes these words in the three boxes at the bottom of the handouts. They tear this strip off and hand it to you. You mix the strips up and redistribute them. Everyone now works individually to write a short story using these words. They should write this first in rough and then copy it into the middle box on their handouts. Circulate to give help and encouragement and stress that the stories need not be long or complicated or realistic. Allow about 15 minutes for this.

Now put people into colour groups so that all those who have written a story with red words sit together, etc. They read all the stories for another colour, for example blue, and comment on them, choosing one or two that are particularly successful to read out to the class.

Conclusion *(5 minutes)*

Write the headings *happy colours* and *sad colours* on the board and invite the class to say which colours go in each list. Does everyone agree on the effect of certain colours or is it personal?

Homework

Choose a colour (not one of the four worked on) and give the class three words connected with this colour. They all write a short story and you can talk about the different versions in a subsequent lesson.

56

17 Colours

RED	WHITE

BLUE	GREEN

My colour: ....   My words: ...., ..., ...

My story:

---

word 1	word 2	word 3

Teacher's notes

18 An English weekend

Aim	To write a simple letter asking for further information. To write a simple publicity flyer (for a language course).
Preparation	Copy the handout on page 59 – one copy per student.
(Optional)	Bring in one or two advertisements for language courses.

Introduction *(5 minutes)*

Introduce the idea of language courses by reading out two of the advertisements you have found and asking students which they prefer and/or by saying that you would like to learn a new foreign language and asking for advice on where to go.

Presentation *(10 minutes)*

Give out the handouts and read the advertisement for the English conversation weekend. Draw students' attention to the useful vocabulary, for example: *conversation, tutor, grammar, vocabulary, confidence, practice, talk, games,* etc. Ask them to choose the three most important features of a successful course and rank these 1, 2, 3. See how far students agree and ask what else they would add to the list, for example listening, reading, tests, homework, etc.

Practice 1 *(15 minutes)*

Point out that the advertisement gives very little concrete information – it doesn't mention price, level, number of participants, etc. – and that you need to write for further details. Students work in pairs to think of what further information they would need before reserving a place on such a course and decide on the four most important questions. They then insert those questions into the letter to Ms Hardy. Circulate to give help and advice and then invite some students to read out their letters. You might like to write a model on the board.

Practice 2 *(15 minutes)*

Ms Hardy had so few students that the course was cancelled! So where did she go wrong? Students now work together in small groups (three to four students) to redesign the leaflet. They decide what would encourage more people to register and what extra information they should give. They then rewrite the leaflet, keeping to the basic short format given. The results can be read out, put up on the walls or passed from group to group for appreciation and comment.

Conclusion *(5 minutes)*

What picture would they put on the leaflet? (A photo of Ms Hardy, of the college, of students? A cartoon?)

Homework

Produce a short publicity leaflet for the English course of their dreams!

18 An English weekend

ENGLISH CONVERSATION
Tutor: Angela Hardy
23–25 June

- Do you want to speak good English?
- Do you need more confidence and practice?
- Spend an English weekend at Williams College!
- We will work on vocabulary and grammar, talk together and play games.
- Comfortable rooms with breakfast and dinner provided.

Write now to Ms A. Hardy, Williams College, to reserve your place.

Dear Ms Hardy,

I am interested in attending your English conversation weekend from 23 to 25 June and I would be grateful if you could give me some further information.

Firstly, ...
....
....
....
and ....
....
....

Secondly, ...
....
....
....

And finally, ...
....
....

I look forward to hearing from you soon.
Yours sincerely,

From *Instant Lessons 1 Elementary* edited by Peter Watcyn-Jones © Penguin Books 2000

Teacher's notes

19 The last chocolate cake

Aim	To practise writing simple direct and indirect speech, producing a short dialogue and article on the same incident.
Preparation	Copy the handout on page 61 – one copy per student.

Introduction *(5 minutes)*

Talk about the last time you went shopping and were unable to get what you wanted because it was sold out. How do students feel when this happens? Try to elicit some vocabulary such as *very angry, furious, upset,* etc.

Presentation *(10 minutes)*

Give out the handout and read the facts about the incident. Ask students to suggest as many reasons for this as they can, for example that it was her son's birthday, that the man was rude to her, that the woman loves chocolate, etc.

Practice 1 *(15 minutes)*

Students work in pairs to write the actual conversation between the man and the woman. Note that this has a beginning and an end and is limited to six exchanges. Then each pair acts out their version for the class, as dramatically as possible.

Practice 2 *(15 minutes)*

Now students work as reporters and write up the same incident as a newspaper article. Draw their attention to the fact that they should report the conversation using reported speech and suggest some suitable verbs: *she asked, he replied, she demanded, he refused, she explained, he complained,* etc.

They should also give the man and woman names, ages and professions and give a few more details about the incident.
Students can work individually or in pairs and the finished articles could be passed round or you could read a selection out to the class.

Conclusion *(5 minutes)*

What happened afterwards? Ask half the group to suggest happy endings and the other half unhappy ones. For example:
The woman made a big chocolate cake and gave it to the man to apologise.
They fell in love and got married.
The man gave up eating chocolate.
The man had to spend a week in hospital and lost his job.
Somebody else took the chocolate cake while they were fighting.

Homework

Give the following facts:
Two women were arrested for fighting in a toy shop because their children wanted the same computer game.
Students can write the conversation or the newspaper article – or both.

19 The last chocolate cake

THE FACTS

A woman punched a man in a London supermarket yesterday because he had taken the last chocolate cake.

THE NEWSPAPER ARTICLE

The woman: Excuse me!

The man: ....

The woman: ....

The man: ....

The woman: ....

The man: Aaaaaah!

CHOCOLATE CAKE CAN BE BAD FOR YOU!

Teacher's notes

20 Trip to the top

Aim:	To understand short biographies and be able to write facts about a person's life, using the past tense and simple appropriate vocabulary.
Preparation:	Copy and cut in half the handout on page 63 – one copy per pair.
(Optional)	Collect a few pictures of film stars to introduce the topic, ideally of Arnold Schwarzenegger and Robert de Niro.

Introduction *(5 minutes)*

Introduce the film stars by coming in with a few pictures or by talking about recent films they starred in. Divide the class into groups and ask them to find out one another's favourite film stars. In a quick whole class round-up, choose the class's favourite star and ask them how much they *really* know about this person.

Presentation and Practice 1 *(25 minutes)*

Write these two sentences on the board:
Michelle Pfeiffer used to work in a supermarket.
Dustin Hoffman's real name is Steven Finklebaum.
followed by these two sentences:
How interesting!
I don't believe it!
Read each sentence and ask selected students to respond with *How interesting!* if they think it's true and with *I don't believe it!* if they don't. (Practise intonation first.) (Answers: TRUE for Pfeiffer and FALSE for Hoffman.)
Divide the class into pairs and give each person one of the profiles. (Each member of the pair must have a different profile and keep it a secret.) Give them time to read their profiles. Any vocabulary you feel may be a problem could be written on the board. Explain that they are going to write three true facts from the profile and make up three more false facts, for example:
Robert de Niro's first part was a lion. (true)
Arnold Schwarzenegger's father was a gym teacher. (false)
Give them time to write the six statements, circulating to give help if needed. Students then take it in turns to read their statements to each other. If the person listening thinks the statement is true, they respond with *How interesting!* and if they think it is false, they respond with *I don't believe it!* Those who responded correctly can be congratulated by the class.

Practice 2 *(15 minutes)*

Explain that it is now time to learn about a famous woman as well and that you are going to read them a very short account of Demi Moore's early life. They have to listen carefully and then afterwards they are going to try to write down everything they remember. Write any difficult words and names on the board.
Demi Moore was born on November 11, 1962 in the USA and was called Demi after a hair product in a magazine. She had a difficult childhood and moved house a lot. She was very thin and shy as a child. At eighteen years old, she had her first part in a television programme called 'General Hospital' and she made her first film at nineteen. At twenty-eight she married Bruce Willis and starred in the hit film 'Ghost'. Now she has three children and is one of the world's most highly paid actresses.
Students first try, working individually, to write everything they remember. They then work with a partner to fill in any gaps and then with another pair to produce a final text. Each group chooses a spokesperson to read their text out to the class and groups who have remembered everything can be congratulated.

Conclusion *(5 minutes)*

Discuss what makes a good film star. Is there some special star quality? Are there any disadvantages to a life of fame and fortune?

Homework

A short biography of a famous person, or an imaginary biography.

20 Trip to the top

ARNOLD SCHWARZENEGGER

Arnold Schwarzenegger was born in a small village in Austria on July 30th, 1947. His father was the chief of police and was very strict. Arnold enjoyed all sports and started bodybuilding at the age of fourteen. He trained for three hours a day, every day, and became an instructor at a health club at the age of nineteen. When he was twenty, he became the youngest Mr Universe in history! After that he became a US citizen and made his first film: **Hercules Goes to New York**. In the years to come, he became a famous film star and played The Terminator twice. Now he has three children and lots of money, and he lives in Hollywood.

3 TRUE facts:

3 FALSE facts:

Robert de Niro

Robert de Niro was born on August 17th, 1943. Both his parents were painters. His father was also called Robert de Niro. He was well behaved at school and loved comic books and going to the cinema. He first acted when he was ten years old and played the part of a lion. From this age he knew he wanted to be an actor. He was in a gang with some Italian kids and his nickname was Bobby Milk. At the age of twenty-four he had his first film role and he won his first Oscar at the age of thirty-one for his role in *The Godfather Part 2*. Now he is one of the best actors in Hollywood and stars in many films.

3 TRUE facts: 3 FALSE facts:

Grammar: Lessons 21–30

21 Present Simple

Aim:	To introduce and practise the form and use of the Present Simple (positive).
Preparation:	Activity A: Copy the handout on page 65 – one copy per student. Activity B: Copy and cut up the cards on page 65 – one set per group. Activity C: Copy and cut up the cards on page 67 – one set per pair/group.

Introduction *(5 minutes)*

Introduce the topic by talking about yourself. For example:
I get up at seven. I drink coffee at breakfast. I walk to school at nine o'clock. I go home at five. I have dinner at seven. I watch the news on TV in the evenings. I go to bed at eleven.
As you do this, write the predicate, i.e. the sentence without the subject *I*, on the board. Now pick out a few individual students. Name the students in turn and in each case point to one of the activities on the board, for example, *get up*. Then say: *James, you get up at ...*
When James completes the sentence, go to another student, point to another activity and get that student to say what s/he does.

Presentation *(15 minutes)*

Start by saying again: *I get up at seven.* Write the whole sentence on the board. Then add: *every day.* Stress to the students that this is a regular habit. Now ask individual students about their habits: *John, what time do you get up every day?* Write John's answer on the board: *John gets up at eight.* Then ask another student the same question, and write up his/her reply.
You can vary the questions, such as: *What do you have for breakfast? How do you come to school?* etc., but gradually build up the statements on the board so that you have all the persons of the verb (*Rita and John, you both get up at eight,* etc.).Then say to the whole class: *Every day, we come to school.* Show by gesture that you are including yourself. When you have put all the statements on the board so that you show all persons of the verb, underline the *s* of the third person singular.

Say that this form is used for regular events or habits and stress the *s* on the third person singular. Draw attention to the *es* with *go* and mention other verbs which do the same, such as *do, wash, miss,* etc. Try to draw a rule from the students, i.e. verbs ending with a vowel, *s, ch* or *sh* add *-es* for the third person singular. Now get the students to question each other in pairs. They have the list of habits on the board, but write up the skeleton questions: *What time do you ...? What do you have ...? How do you ...?* After a few minutes, ask some of the students what they have found out: *John, how does Rita come to school? Anne, what time does David go to bed?,* etc. Stress the *s* on the verb form.

Practice *(20 minutes)*

Activity A Students work individually. Before they do the exercise, check and explain any necessary vocabulary. When they have done the exercise, check orally.

Activity B Get the students into small groups. Give each group a set of cards. The cards are placed in two piles (subject cards and predicate cards) face down on the table. Students now take it in turns to pick up one card from pile 1 and one card from pile 2, which they make into a complete sentence. For example, if the cards are *Jack* and *speak French*, the student would answer: *Jack speaks French.* Then the other students in the group decide if the sentence is correct. Before starting, demonstrate with one group first. If correct, the student keeps the cards. If incorrect, the cards are placed at the bottom of the piles to be used again.

(continued on page 66)

Key

A 1 like 2 lives 3 goes 4 come 5 clean 6 starts
   7 writes 8 rises 9 snows 10 plays

B If one of the following cards is picked from pile 2 – Sam, Jessie, Jack, Olivia, Ben – then the verbs must end with -s. Note that for *wash, miss* and *watch*, the verb will end in *-es*, which should be pronounced as /ɪz/.

(continued on page 66)

64 Teacher's notes

21 Present Simple

A Complete the sentences by putting the verb into the correct form.

1 Tom and Kristin (like)..................... pizzas.
2 Mary (live)..................... in Singapore.
3 Romi (go)..................... to Italy for her holidays.
4 They (come)..................... to work at nine o'clock.
5 We (clean)..................... the car on Sundays.
6 The film (start)..................... at 7.30.
7 John (write)..................... to his family once a month.
8 The sun (rise)..................... in the east.
9 It (snow)..................... a lot in Canada.
10 He (play)..................... tennis every Saturday.

B Card pile 1:

play football at weekends	wash the dishes	live near the school	speak French	cook the dinner
like pizza	miss the bus every morning	paint pictures in the park	watch TV in the evenings	work in an office

Card pile 2:

Sam	Kieran and Chloe	Jessie	I	You
Jack	Adam and Rob	Olivia	Ben	We

From *Instant Lessons 1 Elementary* edited by Peter Watcyn-Jones © Penguin Books 2000

Teacher's notes

Conclusion *(10 minutes)*

Activity C Cut out the squares to make cards. In pairs or groups, the students match a phrase from those round the sides of each square with that of another square. They see how many sentences they can make. Students may enjoy making up absurd sentences such as *The cats drive a big car*. You should accept this.

Homework

Students write some short sentences about themselves, their families or another member of the class.

Key

C *Possible answers:*
Alice: goes to the cinema on Friday/runs in the park/likes milk/gets up early/reads women's magazines.
Jim and Kate: play football on Sunday/eat meat/like films/live in Chile/drive a big car.
We: speak good English/play football on Sunday/eat meat/like films/live in Chile/ drive a big car.
I: speak good English/play football on Sunday/eat meat/like films/live in Chile/drive a big car.
You: speak good English/eat meat/live in Chile/drive a big car.

Mrs Bailey: drinks coffee at breakfast/runs in the park/likes milk/gets up early/reads women's magazines.
She: drinks coffee at breakfast/goes to the cinema on Friday/runs in the park/likes milk/reads women's magazines.
The cats: speak good English/play football on Sunday/like films/live in Chile/drive a big car.

21 Present Simple (continued)

C

I	likes milk
We	runs in the park
Alice	drinks coffee at breakfast
Jim and Kate	speak good English
Mrs Bailey	eat meat
She	gets up early
The cats	play football on Saturday
You	goes to the cinema on Friday
Mr Warren	drive a big car
They	reads women's magazines
Lucy	like films
Noah and Rachel	live in Chile

Teacher's notes

22 Present Simple: interrogative and negative forms

Aim	To introduce and practise the interrogative and negative forms of the Present Simple.
Preparation	Activities A and C: Copy the handouts on pages 69 and 71 – one copy per student. Activity B: Copy and cut up the cards on page 69 – one set per group.

Introduction (5 minutes)

Introduce the topic by talking about things you like, things you do regularly, or things you own. For example: *I like bananas. I walk to school every day. I have three dogs.*
As you do this, ask one or two of the students if they like, do or have the same things. For example: *Do you like bananas? Do you walk to school every day? Do you have three dogs?*
As you make the statements and then ask the questions, write them on the board. Accept one word answers *Yes* or *No*.
Then get the students to work in pairs asking each other similar questions.

Presentation (15 minutes)

Explain that you are practising the question and negative forms of the Present Simple. Ask the students what they have found out about each other and thus expand your table on the board to include the negative forms:
Teacher: *X, does Y walk to school every day?*
Student: *No.*
Teacher: *Ah! Y doesn't walk to school every day.*
At first, you should expect only one word answers which you have to expand. Some students may, however, like to give complete answers. In this case, it will be unnecessary to give the complete answer yourself each time.

Obviously you are, from time to time, going to get a positive answer. Accept it and move on to another question.
Now ask some students some *wh-* questions. For example: *Ruth, where do you live? Joe, when do you get up in the morning? Francis, what do you do in the evenings?*
Write the questions on the board. Then get the students to work in pairs asking each other.

Practice (20 minutes)

Activity A Hand out the questionnaire and get the students to work in pairs, asking the questions and writing down their partners' answers in their full form. When they have been working for a short time, ask them what they have found out. For example: *A, tell me something B doesn't do. B, tell me some things you don't do.*
Put some answers on the board; include the first and second person answers.

Activity B The students works in groups. Each student in turn takes a card from the pile. If the phrase has a question mark (?) after it, they must make a question. If it has NO after it, they must make a negative sentence. Give a short demonstration by taking the first few cards from one group.

(continued on page 70)

Key

A Do you go to bed early?
Do you like poetry?
Do you speak English well?
Do you do a lot of exercise?
Do you have a computer?
Do you wash the dishes?
Do you play football?
Do you watch pop videos?
Do you listen to jazz music?
Do you kiss animals?
Do you enjoy space films?
Do you ride an elephant to school?
B Do I need you?
I don't like meat.
Where does the sun rise?
Does the river Amazon flow through Brazil?
The stars don't shine in the morning.

What does Mark teach?
It doesn't rain a lot in Australia.
Bruce doesn't write interesting books.
Where do Lynn and Ian live?
Do you work at home?
You don't work very hard.
Gisela doesn't live in Berlin.
When does the train arrive?
Birds don't fly west in winter.
We don't have a lot of animals at home.
Does Los Angeles have cold winters?
Do you play chess?
Do they drive fast?
We don't visit our friends every Sunday.
What does that company make?

(continued on page 70)

22 Present Simple: interrogative and negative forms

A Ask your partner questions using the prompts below. Write down his/her answers. For example:

Do you go to bed early?   Yes, I do.

Question	Answer	Question	Answer
go to bed early		play football	
like poetry		watch pop videos	
speak English well		listen to jazz music	
do a lot of exercise		kiss animals	
have a computer		enjoy space films	
wash the dishes		ride an elephant to school	

B

I need you (?)	I like meat (NO)	The sun rises (Where?)	The river Amazon flows through Brazil (?)
The stars shine in the morning (NO)	Mark teaches (What?)	It rains a lot in Australia (NO)	Bruce writes interesting books (NO)
Lynn and Ian live (Where?)	You work at home (?)	You work very hard (NO)	Gisela lives in Berlin (NO)
The train arrives (When?)	Birds fly west in winter (NO)	We have a lot of animals at home (NO)	Los Angeles has cold winters (?)
You play chess (?)	They drive fast (?)	We visit our friends every Sunday (NO)	That company makes (What?)

From *Instant Lessons 1 Elementary* edited by Peter Watcyn-Jones © Penguin Books 2000

Teacher's notes

Conclusion (10 minutes)

Activity C Students work on the substitution tables for consolidation, in pairs or groups of three. This can become a competition to see which pair/group can make the most sentences.

Homework

Students write ten sentences about their partner that they have found out from the student questionnaire. They might also write ten questions they would like to ask each other.

Key

C *Some possible questions:*
  Where do you work?
  Where do Liam and Leah play football?
  Does Elisa work in an office?
  Do you go to the cinema every week?
  When do you get up?
  Do you get up early?
  When does Jacob play football?
  Do you play football?
  Does Elisa have television?
  Where do we play football?

Some possible negative sentences:
  I don't live in London.
  You don't walk to school.
  Daniel doesn't like meat.
  Hannah doesn't eat fish.
  We don't have a television.
  George and Esther don't walk to school.
  Hannah doesn't have children.
  Daniel doesn't talk to his neighbour.
  You don't like children.
  I don't buy fish.

22 Present Simple: interrogative and negative forms (continued)

C 1 Make as many correct questions as you can. You can begin the question either with *Where* or *When* or with *Do* or *Does*. If you begin with *Where* or *When*, leave out the phrases in the last column. For example:

Where do Liam and Leah work?
Do Liam and Leah work in an office?

where	do	you	go	in an office
when	does	Jacob	play	a guitar
		Elisa	get up	football
		we	work	television
		Liam and Leah	have	to the cinema every week
			watch	early

2 Make as many negative sentences as you can.

I	doesn't	like	children
you	don't	eat	in London
Daniel		walk	fish
Hannah		talk	a television
we		live	to school
George and Esther		have	meat
		buy	to his neighbour

From *Instant Lessons 1 Elementary* edited by Peter Watcyn-Jones © Penguin Books 2000

Teacher's notes

23 The article

Aim	To introduce and contrast the use of the definite article (*the*) and the indefinite article (*a/an*).
Preparation	Copy the handouts on pages 73 and 75 – one copy per student.

Introduction *(5 minutes)*

Bring in a bag of objects, for example an apple, a postcard, a pencil, a book and an orange. Be sure that the name of some of the objects begins with a vowel and of others with a consonant.

Take the things one by one from the bag and ask the students what they are: *What's this?* If they give just one word answers, for example *orange, pencil,* complete the answer: *It's an orange. It's a pencil.*

Write the full answer on the board. If an answer is not forthcoming quickly, give it yourself and write it on the board. Underline the indefinite article and where it is *an,* link the *n* to the initial vowel of the following word: *an apple.*

Hand the objects to various students and get them to ask other students: *What's this?*

Presentation *(15 minutes)*

Put two columns on the board:
A/AN   THE
Explain that you are looking at the uses of *a/an* and *the.* Now go through the objects again. For example:
Teacher: *What's this?*
Student: *It's an apple.*
When the student has answered correctly, put the apple on your desk or in front of a student and then ask another student:
Where's the apple?
Write this on the board, underlining *the* each time.

You can vary the question by giving the object to another student and asking: *Who's got the ...?* Now write the dialogue on the board, for example:
What's this?
It's an apple.
Who's got the apple?
Steve's got the apple.

Explain that at the first mention you use *a/an,* but when you talk about the object again, you use *the.* Write 1 against *a/an* and 2 against *the.* Ask the students to give you something. Then hand out the objects you've received randomly to the students and get them to practise using the dialogue as a model.

Practice *(20 minutes)*

Activity A Working in pairs, they place the words or phrases in the appropriate column. Check answers orally with the whole class.

Activity B Let the students work in pairs to fill in the gaps in the dialogue with *a/an/the.* Explain any new vocabulary, such as the names of the animals. When they have finished, get some of the pairs to act out the dialogue.

(continued on page 74)

Key

A A: pencil, clock, car, man, room, boiled egg, village, green apple, house, town house, picture, horse, town
AN: orange, egg, old man, Italian town, Albanian village, apple, old picture

B 1 a   2 A   3 the   4 a   5 the   6 the

(continued on page 74)

23 The article

A Put the words or phrases below into the correct column.

A	AN

orange   pencil   clock   car
egg   man   old man   room
Italian town boiled egg   village   Albanian village
apple   green apple   house   town house
picture   old picture   horse   town

B Complete the dialogue by putting in *the* or *a*.

John: Is that (1) _____ lion over there?

Tessa: (2) _____ lion?

John: Yes. I think it's (3) _____ lion that escaped from the zoo. He's called Rory.

Tessa: Rubbish. But I can see (4) _____ zebra.

John: It's Deborah, (5) _____ zebra that escaped from the zoo.

Tessa: How do you know?

John: They've lost a lion and a zebra. It was on (6) _____ news.

From *Instant Lessons 1 Elementary* edited by Peter Watcyn-Jones © Penguin Books 2000

Teacher's notes

Activity C Let the students work in pairs to fill in the gaps with *a/the*. Explain any new vocabulary, such as *din* (a noise), *tin* (a metal), *balloon*. When they have finished, get the class to read the poems chorally.

Activity D The students look back at Activities A, B and C and try to work out what the rules for the use of *a/an/the* are.

Conclusion *(10 minutes)*

Activity E Students work in pairs to complete the text. Make sure they understand the words *elephant*, *keeper* and *trunk*. Check orally.

Homework

Students write some short sentences describing what is in a room at home and describing the object they've mentioned. Give them an example:
In my room, there is a desk. The desk is big.

Key

C 1 a 2 a 3 a 4 The 5 The 6 an 7 a 8 a 9 the 10 a 11 a 12 The 13 The

D The rules to check are:
1 A or AN – when a person or thing is first mentioned
2 A – if the following word begins with a consonant
3 AN – if the following word begins with a vowel
4 THE – when the person or thing has been mentioned before
5 THE – if the person or thing is the only one of its kind

E 1 a/the 2 The 3 a 4 An 5 a/the 6 the 7 The 8 A 9 the 10 the 11 the 12 A 13 The 14 the 15 the 16 the 17 the 18 the 19 a 20 the

23 The article (continued)

C Complete the poems by inserting *the*, *a* or *an*.

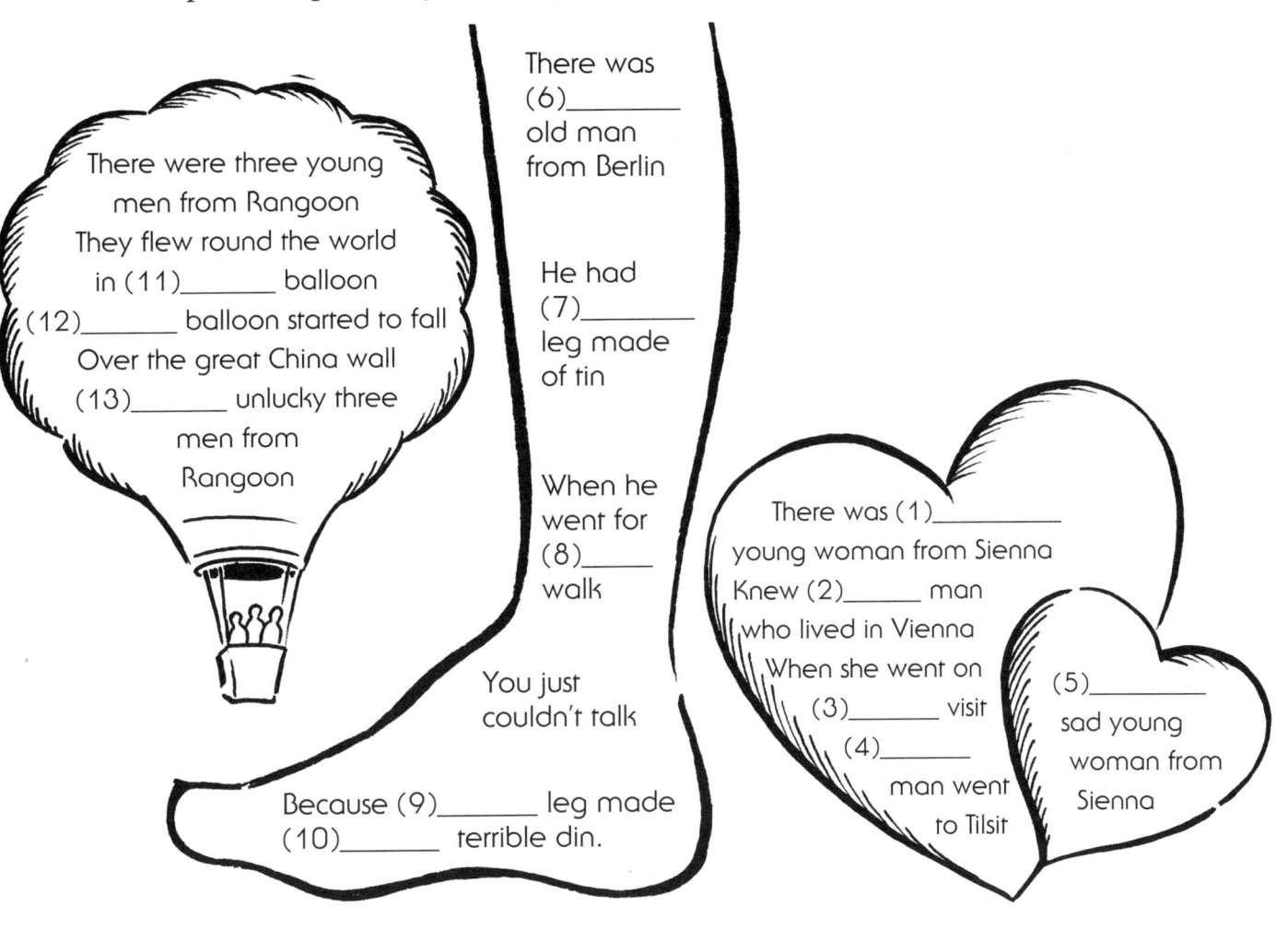

There were three young men from Rangoon
They flew round the world
in (11)_____ balloon
(12)_____ balloon started to fall
Over the great China wall
(13)_____ unlucky three men from Rangoon

There was (6)_____ old man from Berlin

He had (7)_____ leg made of tin

When he went for (8)_____ walk

You just couldn't talk

Because (9)_____ leg made (10)_____ terrible din.

There was (1)_____ young woman from Sienna
Knew (2)_____ man who lived in Vienna
When she went on (3)_____ visit
(4)_____ man went to Tilsit

(5)_____ sad young woman from Sienna

D In groups, look at your answers to Activities A, B and C, and make some rules for the use of *the*, *a* and *an*.

E Complete the story by putting in *the* or *a/an*.

On Fridays, John always gets (1) _____ bus from his home to his tennis club. (2) _____ bus is usually on time, but last Friday there was (3) _____ problem. (4) _____ elephant escaped from (5) _____ local zoo and sat down in front of (6) _____ bus. (7) _____ elephant was tired. (8) _____ keeper from (9) _____ zoo came. But (10) _____ keeper was new and (11) _____ elephant didn't know him and so didn't move. (12) _____ man on the bus tried to help. (13) _____ elephant didn't like (14) _____ man. He lifted (15) _____ man with his trunk and waved him in the air. The people on (16) _____ bus were very frightened and started to get off. John got off last. Immediately (17) _____ elephant put (18) _____ man down, got up and waved his trunk at John. The elephant was pleased to see John. John always gave him (19) _____ cake when he went to (20) _____ zoo.

From *Instant Lessons 1 Elementary* edited by Peter Watcyn-Jones © Penguin Books 2000

Teacher's notes

24 *Some/any* and countable/uncountable

Aim	To show how *some* and *any* are used, and to introduce countable and uncountable nouns.
Preparation	Copy the handout on page 77 – one copy per student.

Introduction *(5 minutes)*

Introduce the topic by asking students if they've got things or if they want anything:
Have you got any books here?
Do you want any money?
Expect the simple answer *Yes* or *No*.
Write the questions on the board. Then the students work in pairs, taking it in turns to ask and answer questions.

Presentation *(15 minutes)*

Write *some* and *any* on the board, then ask the question again: *Have you got any money?* As you do so, underline *any* and the question mark. When the student says *Yes*, write the complete answer on the board: *Yes, I've got some money.* Now underline *Yes* and *some*.
Now ask a question where you would expect a negative answer, for example: *Are there any horses in the class?* When the student answers *No*, write the complete answer on the board: *No, there aren't any horses in the class.* Now underline *No* and *any*.
Explain that you use *any* for questions and negative answers and *some* for positive answers. Then students work in pairs and ask each other similar questions.
Now ask your question again: *Are there any horses in the class?* Then ask a question with an uncountable noun, for example: *Is there any water on the floor?*
Write the questions on the board and underline the initial verb and show that in the first case you have used a singular verb and in the second case a plural verb. Tell the students that you can count things such as *apples, bottles, horses, men, women,* etc., but not others, such as *bread, cheese, coffee, furniture, information, money, water,* etc. Get them to suggest things you can count and things you can't count and write them in two columns on the board.

Practice *(20 minutes)*

Activity A The students work individually. Check this at the end and discuss the rule with them again: *any* for questions and negative answers and *some* for positive answers.

Activity B Students do this in groups. Make it a timed exercise and see which group gets most words in the time. First check for words they might not know, such as *basket, canal, cash, decision, joke, van,* etc.

Conclusion *(10 minutes)*

Activity C The students work in pairs to match a phrase in column 1 with one in column 2. Check new vocabulary, such as *llama, shark,* etc. Check orally when they have finished.

Homework

Activity D It may be necessary to explain why *news* is uncountable. It is better to do this after they have done the homework.

Key

A 1 any 2 any 3 some 4 any 5 some 6 some
  7 some 8 any 9 any 10 any, some
B Countable: bank, canal, decision, group, joke, year, thought, van, language, office, child, newspaper, machine, basket, holiday
  Uncountable: clothing, education, furniture, air, cash, money, hope, paper, cheese, information, water, tea, work, fruit, coffee
C *(in any order)*
  There is some ice cream in the fridge.
  Is there any cheese?
  There are some interesting pictures in the museum.
  There aren't any new computer games in the shop.
  Are there any sharks in the sea near here?
  There are some very noisy dogs in this street.
  There isn't any good furniture nowadays.
  There isn't any homework tonight.
  There is some money on the table.
  Are there any llamas in the zoo?
D 1 any 2 is 3 some, any 4 Is 5 are 6 Is 7 any
  8 some 9 some, any 10 Are

76

24 Some/any and countable/uncountable

A Fill in the gaps with *some* or *any*.

1 Have you got _____ biscuits?
2 In Greece, they haven't had _____ rain for months.
3 It's a long train journey. Get _____ magazines.
4 He's very poor. He hasn't had _____ work for months.
5 She bought _____ shoes at that cheap shop.
6 Give him _____ time. He'll do the work for you.
7 She likes _____ people on this course, but not all of them.
8 Have you got _____ information about a trip to China?
9 They didn't sell _____ tickets for the school concert.
10 Have you got _____ Spanish money? I need _____ pesetas. I'm going to Seville tomorrow.

B Make two columns – COUNTABLE and UNCOUNTABLE – and put the words below in the correct column.

clothing	education	furniture	air	bank	canal
decision	cash	money	group	hope	joke
year	thought	paper	cheese	van	language
office	information	water	tea	work	child
newspaper	fruit	coffee	machine	basket	holiday

C Work in pairs. Match a phrase in column 1 with one in column 2.

1	2
There is	any llamas in the zoo?
Is there	some ice cream in the fridge.
There are	any cheese?
There aren't	some interesting pictures in the museum.
Are there	any new computer games in the shop.
There are	any sharks in the sea near here?
There isn't	some very noisy dogs in this street.
There isn't	any good furniture nowadays.
There is	any homework tonight.
Are there	some money on the table.

D Fill in the gaps in the exercise below.

1 I don't want _____ sugar in my coffee.
2 There _____ some milk in the fridge.
3 Give me _____ potatoes; but I don't want _____ carrots.
4 _____ there any life on Mars?
5 There _____ some interesting new films at the cinema this week.
6 _____ there any interesting news today?
7 Did you take _____ money from this drawer?
8 You need _____ apples and onions for that recipe.
9 I've got _____ apples, but I don't have _____ onions.
10 _____ there any onions in the garden?

Teacher's notes

25 Past Simple v Past Continuous

Aim	To show how the Past Simple and Past Continuous are used together.
Preparation	Activities A, C and D: Copy the handouts on pages 79 and 81 – one copy per student. Activity B: Copy and cut up the dominoes on page 79 – one set per pair.

Introduction (5 minutes)

Introduce the topic by telling the students what you were doing the previous evening. Tell it as a story which need not be absolutely true. For example: *Yesterday evening, I was watching TV.*
Write this on the board.
While I was watching TV, I heard a lot of noise in the street.
Write this on the board.
While I was listening to the noise, suddenly a brick came through my window.
There is no need to finish the story. Get the students to work in pairs and ask them to think of the next two events in the story. Then hear what some of them have thought of and write their sentences on the board.

Presentation (15 minutes)

Underline the two forms of the verbs on the board and explain that you are looking at the difference between the use of the two forms of the verb.
Now go back to the beginning of your story. Draw a time line:

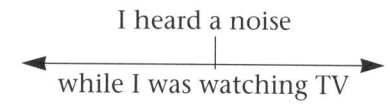

```
            I heard a noise
        ←―――――|―――――→
         while I was watching TV
```

Show how the *I heard a noise* interrupts *watching TV*; that *I heard a noise* is a short, immediate action, whereas *watching TV* goes on for a long time.

Now get students to add to your story. Then ask them to take one of the sentences in the story and draw their own time line. Encourage them to develop a fun, even absurd story.

Practice (20 minutes)

Activity A The students do this individually. Check orally.

Activity B Play the game in pairs. Give each pair a set of dominoes and explain that they have to match the second part of one domino to the first part of another to make a full sentence. They should arrange the dominoes to make a square. Put this shape guide on the board to help them:

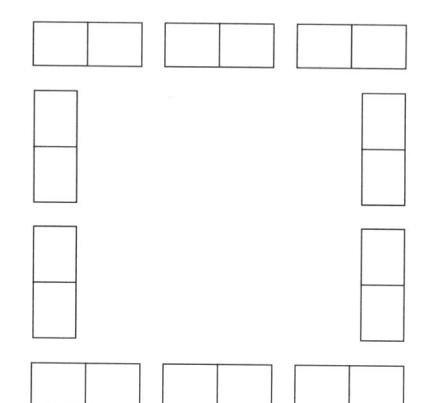

(continued on page 80)

Key

A 1 was living   2 met   3 asked   4 were playing, kicked   5 saw   6 broke   7 was calling, ran away   8 knew
   9 was painting, happened   10 drew

B Jim and Kath were walking in the park // when the rain started
   when he won the lottery // he went on a luxury holiday
   she was learning how to send an email // when the computer stopped working
   while Lilian was climbing a tree // she fell and hurt her leg
   they were sleeping in bed // when there was a noise in the living room
   we were watching the news // when we saw Ella on TV
   while he was writing // he dreamt of becoming a famous novelist
   he was listening to the radio // while he was washing the car
   while the fire fighters were trying to stop the fire // everyone in the house escaped safely
   the man was breaking a window // when the police arrived

(continued on page 80)

25 Past Simple v Past Continuous

A Write the correct form of the verb.

1. Gerry got married while he (live) in Madrid.
2. He (meet) Isabel while he was working in a record store.
3. She (ask) him to marry her on 29th February.
4. The boys (play) football on the beach when one of them (kick) the ball into the drinks stand.
5. The owner of the stand (see) the incident.
6. The ball (break) a lot of bottles and glasses.
7. While the owner (call) the police, the boys (run away).
8. But the owner (know) the boys.
9. An artist (paint) on the beach when the incident (happen).
10. He (draw) a picture of the boys for the police.

B Work in pairs and play dominoes. Put the dominoes together to make complete sentences.

when the police arrived	Jim and Kath were walking in the park	he went on a luxury holiday	she was learning how to send an email
she fell and hurt her leg	they were sleeping in bed	everyone in the house escaped safely	the man was breaking a window
when the rain started	when he won the lottery	when there was a noise in the living room	we were watching the news
when the computer stopped working	while Lilian was climbing a tree	when we saw Ella on TV	while he was writing
while he was washing the car	while the fire fighters were trying to stop the fire	he dreamt of becoming a famous novelist	he was listening to the radio

From *Instant Lessons 1 Elementary* edited by Peter Watcyn-Jones © Penguin Books 2000

Teacher's notes

Conclusion *(10 minutes)*

Activity C The students work in pairs. Encourage them to work quickly by making this a competition to see which pair finishes first. You may need to explain that *I.T.* means *Information Technology* – work with computers. Check orally when they have finished.

Homework

Activity D Check orally in the next lesson.

Key

C 1 In 1990, Tony left school (and started travelling round the world).
   2 In 1993, Lucy was training as a teacher.
   3 In 1993, Tony was studying I.T.
   4 In 1996, Lucy was teaching in Manchester and met Rob.
   5 In 1992, Tony met Maria.
   6 In 1998, Lucy was working with Rob in Brazil.
   7 In 1996, Tony married Maria.
   8 In 1999, Tony was living in London and became a father.
   9 In 1999, Lucy met Angelo.
   10 In 2000, Lucy married Angelo.

D 1 Where was Paolo standing when the wall collapsed?
      What happened while Paolo was standing on the wall?
   2 What happened while Maggie was working late?
      What was Maggie doing when the thieves broke into the office?
   3 What was Brad doing when it started to rain?
      What happened while Brad was teaching Diego the rules of cricket?
   4 What were Carlos and Anna doing when the accident happened?
      What happened while Carlos and Anna were cycling to Wales?
   5 What was Kate doing when the thief stole her bag?
      What happened while Kate was walking along the street?
   6 What did his wife do while Tony was taking the dog for a walk?
      What was Tony doing while his wife cooked the dinner?
   7 What was Jane doing when she hurt her knee?
      What happened while Jane was training for the Rome marathon?
   8 What happened while they were visiting their aunt?
      What were they doing when the fire started?
   9 What did Lee do while he was waiting to go to university?
      When did Lee work in Australia?
   10 What did Tom do while Hannah was talking about her new Nintendo game?
      What was Hannah doing when Tom fell asleep?

25 Past Simple v Past Continuous *(continued)*

C Work in pairs. Complete the sentences using the information in the table.

LUCY	
1984–90	At school
1991	Work in Africa
1992-95	Train as a teacher
1995-97	Teach in Manchester
1996	Meet Rob
1997-2000	Work with Rob in Brazil
1999	Meet Angelo
2000	Marry Angelo

TONY	
1982–90	At school
1988	Learn to drive
1990–91	Travel round the world
1991–94	Study I.T.
1992	Meet Maria
1994–97	Work for IBM in New York
1996	Marry Maria
1997–2001	Live in London
1999	Become a father

For example:
In 1985, Tony *was going to school*.
In 1991, Lucy *worked in Africa*.

1 In 1990, Tony ....
2 In 1993, Lucy ....
3 In 1993, Tony ....
4 In 1996, Lucy ....
   and ....
5 In 1992, Tony ....
6 In 1998, Lucy ....
7 In 1996, Tony ....
8 In 1999, Tony ....
   and ....
9 In 1999, Lucy ....
10 In 2000, Lucy ....

D Write two possible questions for the following statements.
For example:

Andy saw the accident when he was having lunch in the restaurant.
What did Andy see when he was having lunch in the restaurant?
What was Andy doing when he saw the accident?

1 Paolo was standing on the wall when it collapsed.
2 Maggie was working late when the thieves broke into the office.
3 Brad was teaching Diego the rules of cricket when it started to rain.
4 Carlos and Anna were cycling to Wales when the accident happened.
5 Kate was walking along the street when the thief stole her bag.
6 Tony was taking the dog for a walk while his wife cooked the dinner.
7 Jane was training for the Rome marathon when she hurt her knee.
8 The fire started while they were visiting their aunt.
9 Lee worked in Australia while he was waiting to go to university.
10 Tom fell asleep while Hannah was talking about her new Nintendo game.

From *Instant Lessons 1 Elementary* edited by Peter Watcyn-Jones © Penguin Books 2000

Teacher's notes

26 Frequency adverbs

Aim	To understand the relative meanings of the following frequency adverbs: *always, usually, often, sometimes, never* and their unmarked position in a statement. Also the interrogative use of *ever*.
Preparation	Activity A: Copy and cut up the cards on page 83 – one set per group of four or five. Activities B, C and D: Copy the handout on page 85 – one copy per student.

Introduction *(5 minutes)*

Introduce the topic by talking about yourself. For example:
I always play football on Saturday.
I never watch TV on Tuesday, because there aren't any good programmes on.
Write these two sentences on the board. Now ask the students:
What do you on Saturday? Do you always ... on Saturday?
Get the students to work in pairs asking each other the above questions.

Presentation *(15 minutes)*

Write the adverbs on the board, one under the other, and explain that you want to know what they mean and how they are used in a sentence. Then make a table:

ALWAYS   x x x x x x x x x x (100%)
USUALLY   x x x x x x x (85%)
OFTEN   x x x x x (60%)
SOMETIMES   x x x x (40%)
NEVER   (0%)

Activity A Take out the pile 1 prompt cards and ask the students: *Do you ever ...?*
Then point to the adverb you want included in the answer. Do this as long as necessary to be able to include all the adverbs. Write the question form on the board and point out the use of *ever*. Also write the answers on the board and show that the adverb always comes just before the main verb, except with the verb *to be* when it comes after.
When you have done this for the positive answer, repeat for negative answers, showing that the adverb comes after *do not* but before the main verb.
Then put the students into groups of four or five students. Have a set of the prompt cards for each group. There should be two piles: one with the activity and one with the adverbs. One student takes a card from the top of the activity pile and asks another student a question using *ever*. For example: *Do you ever play the trumpet in bed?* The student asked then takes a card from the adverb pile and answers using that adverb. For example: *Yes, I always play the trumpet in bed.* Explain any necessary vocabulary such as *kilt* (a skirt with the family design worn on formal occasions by men in Scotland).

(continued on page 84)

(key on page 84)

26 Frequency adverbs

A Pile 1

play the trumpet in bed	eat spaghetti for breakfast	swim in the river	be late for the class
wear a kilt	dance on the dinner table	climb mountains before breakfast	copy your friend's homework
finish your work on time	enjoy horror films	run with no shoes on	take photographs on your holidays
read sports magazines	play computer games	go for long walks at the weekend	

Pile 2

always	not always	usually	not usually
often	not often	sometimes	never

From *Instant Lessons 1 Elementary* edited by Peter Watcyn-Jones © Penguin Books 2000

Teacher's notes

Practice *(20 minutes)*

Activity B The students do the exercise individually. Check orally.

Activity C Put the students into groups. See how many sentences they can make. You can make this competitive by giving them a time limit, say 5 minutes.

Conclusion *(10 minutes)*

Activity D Students work in pairs to complete the dialogue. Check orally by getting pairs to act out the dialogue.

Homework

Students write five sentences about the people who were in their group using the answers they got from the prompt cards exercise.

Key

B 1 Liam always plays football on Saturdays.
   2 What do you usually do in the holidays?
   3 Gerry is never late.
   4 Joe sometimes works late.
   5 I never liked that picture.
   6 The trains in Germany are usually on time.
   7 Does Angelo often buy flowers for Natasha?
   8 Yes. He always buys them for her at the weekend.
   9 Jake often went for a walk near the lake in the summer.
   10 That book never gives the right answers.

C *Some possible sentences (there will be others):*
   1 John always has his holiday in Italy.
   2 The prince has never been to the cinema.
   3 His friends sometimes forgot his birthday.
   4 You usually get here on time.
   5 Lions always attack rabbits.
   6 Dinner is often late here.
   7 Sally often plays tennis on Thursday.
   8 Rob never rides his bicycle by the canal.
   9 Liz always left the office early.
   10 The river is always crowded in summer.

D ROB: Do you always go to see Gary on Saturday?
   JENNY: Oh, no; but I usually try to see him on either Friday or Saturday.
   ROB: What do you usually do?
   JENNY: Different things. We sometimes go to the cinema, but we often stay at home.
   ROB: Do you sometimes go to the disco?
   JENNY: Oh no! We never go there.
   ROB: Why not?
   JENNY: He doesn't like disco music.
   ROB: I sometimes go. Would you come with me?
   JENNY: All right.

26 Frequency adverbs *(continued)*

B Rewrite the sentences to include the adverbs given.

1. Liam plays football on Saturdays. (always)
2. What do you do in the holidays? (usually)
3. Gerry is late. (never)
4. Joe works late. (sometimes)
5. I liked that picture. (never)
6. The trains in Germany are on time. (usually)
7. Does Angelo buy flowers for Natasha? (often)
8. Yes. He buys them for her at the weekend. (always)
9. Jake went for a walk near the lake in the summer. (often)
10. That book gives the right answers. (never)

C See how many sentences you can make from the words in the box. Each sentence must contain one of the adverbs.

> John is the summer you cinema canal lions usually river his office always bicycle prince birthday often left friends by crowded has Rob get plays never attack sometimes early a late here been rabbits holiday tennis to on rides in Liz time Thursday Italy dinner forgot Sally

D Rob and Jenny are talking about a friend. Put the adverb in the correct place in the sentence. The appropriate adverb is suggested by the percentage at the end of the sentence.

ROB: Do you go to see Gary on Saturday? (100%)
JENNY: Oh, no; but I try to see him on either Friday or Saturday. (85%)
ROB: What do you do? (85%)
JENNY: Different things. We go to the cinema (40%), but we stay at home. (60%)
ROB: Do you go to the disco? (40%)
JENNY: Oh no! We go there. (0%)
ROB: Why not?
JENNY: He doesn't like disco music.
ROB: I go (40%). Would you come with me?
JENNY: All right.

From *Instant Lessons 1 Elementary* edited by Peter Watcyn-Jones © Penguin Books 2000

Teacher's notes

27 Prepositions of time

Aim	To practise the use of *in*, *on* and *at* when talking about time.
Preparation	Copy the handout on page 87 – one copy per student.

Introduction *(5 minutes)*

Introduce the topic by asking individual students the following questions. Write down the replies on the board, underlining the prepositional phrases.
What do you do in the evening?
What do you do on Saturdays?
What do you do at Christmas? (or any other festival as appropriate)
When there is a mistake in the answer in the use of the preposition, tell the student to listen carefully as you repeat the question emphasising the preposition.

Presentation *(15 minutes)*

Explain that you are going to discuss the use of *in*, *on* and *at* as prepositions for time.
Write on the board: *ON for days*. Ask some questions: *What do you do on Saturdays?*
What do you do on Christmas Day?
Write the questions on the board and underline *on*. Point out that with the Present Simple you can say *on Saturday* or *on Saturdays* and this means every Saturday. When, however, you use the past (*What did you do on Saturday?*) you mean the previous Saturday; and when you use the future (*What will you do on Saturday?*) you mean the next Saturday.

Write *AT* on the board. Now ask questions:
What did you do at Easter?
What time do you go to bed at night?
What are you going to do at five o'clock today?

Write the questions on the board and underline *at*.

Write *IN* on the board. Now ask questions:
What do you do in the evening/morning/afternoon?
What did you do in the holidays?
What are you going to do in July?
Write the questions on the board and underline *in*. Point out that we say *in the morning/afternoon/evening*, but *at night*.
Put the students into pairs and get them to ask and answer similar questions.

Practice *(20 minutes)*

Activity A The students work individually. Check answers orally. Then they work in pairs to test each other. Each student in turn says a word and the other says which column the word is in.

Activity B The students work individually to complete the questions. When they have done this they find a partner and ask their questions. Check orally at the end.

Conclusion *(10 minutes)*

Activity C Students work in small groups. Have a time limit of 5 minutes. Check orally and see which group has the most sentences.

Homework

Activity D Students complete this for homework. Check orally in the next lesson.

Key

A

IN	ON	AT
the evening	Wednesday	night
the morning	Saturday	Easter
June	Tuesday evening	Christmas
1996	Monday morning	the weekend
the spring		three o'clock
the holidays		

B *Possible words:*
After IN: the morning, afternoon or evening; the name of a month; the name of a season – spring, summer, autumn or winter; a year
After ON: a day of the week; a part of the day, e.g. on Tuesday morning; a date, e.g. on 21st January; a special day, e.g. on Christmas Day.
After AT: night; a short festive period e.g. Christmas (but not Christmas Day); a time.

C *Possible answers (there will be others):*
1 Harry works at the weekend.
2 The circus came here in August.
3 They didn't go to the theatre on Saturday.
4 Some animals sleep in winter.
5 Tara started her job on 31st March.
6 Joseph left at night.
7 Cameron had an accident on Monday evening.
8 The car broke down on Sunday.
9 Thieves stole Daisy's jewellery on Christmas Day.
10 Megan and Ryan arrived home at 6 o'clock.

D 1 on 2 at 3 in 4 on 5 at 6 in 7 in 8 in 9 in 10 on

27 Prepositions of time

A Work individually. Make three columns and put headings IN, ON and AT. Then put the words below in the appropriate column.

> the evening   Wednesday   the morning   June   1996   night   Saturday
> the spring   Easter   Christmas   the holidays   Tuesday evening
> the weekend   Monday morning   three o'clock

B Work individually to complete the questions. Then, in pairs, ask your questions and write down your partner's answers.

1 What did you do on .... ?
2 What are you going to do in .... ?
3 What were you doing at .... ?
4 Are you going to see the match on .... ?
5 Did you buy those clothes on .... ?
6 Where will you be in .... ?
7 Who won the game on .... ?
8 Did you go to the cinema on .... ?
9 Did you stay at home at .... ?
10 What did you do in .... ?

C How many sentences can you make from the words below? Each sentence must contain a preposition of time. You can use each word only once, except for *on*, *in*, *at*, *to* and *the*.

August	circus	night	Tara	broke down	31st March
on	Harry	Megan	winter	in	left
came	home	had	car	the	they
weekend	at	arrived	here	works	some
didn't	6 o'clock	Monday	Cameron	Joseph	theatre
to	evening	accident	thieves	Christmas Day	her
stole	job	an	jewellery	animals	go
sleep	Saturday	Sunday	and	Ryan	Daisy's

D Complete the sentences below by underlining the correct preposition.

1 I was in the park (on, in, at) Tuesday afternoon.
2 There were a lot of good films on TV (on, in, at) Christmas.
3 John met Gina in Madrid (on, in, at) the summer.
4 Did you see the horses on the beach (on, in, at) Sunday?
5 There were a lot of people at the fair (on, in, at) the weekend.
6 Charlie is a good tennis player, but he won't play (on, in, at) the winter.
7 Maria loves climbing and always goes to the mountains (on, in, at) August.
8 He didn't want to go to the theatre (on, in, at) the afternoon.
9 Beth and Nick love the sun and the sea, so they always go to Australia (on, in, at) January.
10 Laura's paying. She won the lottery (on, in, at) Saturday night.

From *Instant Lessons 1 Elementary* edited by Peter Watcyn-Jones © Penguin Books 2000

Teacher's notes

28 Prepositions of place

Aim	To practise the use of *above, at, behind, by, in, in front of, near, next to, on, opposite* and *under*.
Preparation	Activities A, B, C and E: Copy the handouts on pages 89 and 93 – one copy per student. Activity D: Copy and cut in half the handout on page 91 – one copy per pair.

Introduction *(5 minutes)*

Introduce the topic by telling the following story. As you do so, draw the scene on the board and explain any difficult vocabulary, for example: *terrible mess, shelf, filing cabinet, strange object*, etc.
When Jane arrived in the office, it was a terrible mess. Her desk was in front of the filing cabinet. Her chair was on the other side of the room, opposite her desk. Her computer was under the desk. Behind the filing cabinet there was a small glass bottle, and next to it a strange object. Jane picked up the strange object and put it on the shelf above the filing cabinet, near a vase of flowers.

Write the prepositions in their appropriate places in the picture. Then ask the students various questions, for example:
John, who is sitting behind you?
Maria, where is your pen?
Gemma, where is Joanna sitting? etc.

Presentation *(15 minutes)*

Explain that you are going to practise prepositions of place. Go back to the story and ask the students questions, for example:
Where was Jane's desk?
Where was her computer?
Where was the bottle?
Where did she put the strange object? etc.

Make sure students understand the difference between *opposite/in front of*, *near/next to* and *on/above*. Now ask each student to think of two questions, where the answer will require the use of a preposition. The questions can be about the story, about the classroom or about the town. They ask their questions in open pairs.

Practice *(20 minutes)*

Activity A Get the students to work in groups. They see how many sentences they can make. Make this competitive by giving them a time limit, say 5 minutes.

Activity B The students do this exercise individually. Check orally.

Activity C Again the students work individually. Check orally when they have finished.

(continued on page 90)

Key

A *Possible answers (there will be others):*
1 An old woman lived near there.
2 The station master was standing next to the station.
3 The train stopped under the bridge.
4 Nobody saw the lion behind the tree.
5 Marian planted a lot of roses in her garden.
6 In front of the house was a river.
7 The restaurant was opposite the police station.
8 The telephone is by the door.
9 Jack and Jill stood on the hill.
10 My bicycle was in the cellar.

Possible long sentences:
Jack and Jill stood on the hill near the river and saw Marian in front of the house by the bridge.
Mary and the station master planted the tree opposite the police station next to the restaurant on the hill near the river.

B 1 in 2 at 3 in 4 in 5 on 6 in/behind 7 at 8 on, in

C 1 in 2 next to 3 behind 4 In front of 5 in 6 Behind 7 behind 8 above 9 On 10 at

(continued on page 90)

88

28 Prepositions of place

A In groups, see how many sentences with a preposition you can make from the words below. You must not use any word more than three times, except *a, an, the* and *was*. What is the longest sentence you can make?

under	nobody	house	Marian	standing	was
the	telephone	Jack	stood	cellar	in
next to	in front of	train	bridge	tree	garden
planted	restaurant	there	police station	bicycle	Jill
lived	woman	a	and	an	house
roses	a lot of	stopped	station master	her	is
behind	opposite	near	on	lion	saw
hill	river	by	old	door	station

B Complete the sentences using *at, in, on, under, behind*.

1 Frankie lives .... Mexico.
2 Daisy is .... school today. She will be on holiday next week.
3 The smallest state .... the United States is Rhode Island.
4 In 2000, the Olympic Games were held .... Sydney.
5 He's got a hat .... his head.
6 Matt is hiding .... that large tree.
7 Nicki stayed .... the most expensive hotel in Paris.
8 Put the plates .... the table and the cups .... the cupboard.

C Complete the description of the picture below using the correct preposition: *above, at, behind, in, in front of, next to, on*.

The bride and groom are sitting (1) _____ the open carriage. The bride is sitting (2) _____ the groom. They are sitting (3) _____ the driver. (4) _____ the carriage is a brown horse. The driver is holding a whip (5) _____ his hand.
(6) _____ the carriage there are some trees, and (7) _____ the trees, there are some high mountains. The sky (8) _____ them is very grey. But there is some sun. (9) _____ the grass, (10) _____ the side of the road, you can see the shadow of the carriage.

From *Instant Lessons 1 Elementary* edited by Peter Watcyn-Jones © Penguin Books 2000

Teacher's notes

Conclusion *(10 minutes)*

Activity D The students do this activity in pairs. Give one student in each pair picture 1, and the other picture 2. They have to find the differences in the two pictures. There are ten differences. Check orally when they have finished.

(continued on page 92)

Key

D *The differences in the second picture are:*
1 The cupboard door is closed.
2 The person in the office through the door is sitting on the desk.
3 The vase is a tall one.
4 The pile of papers on the filing cabinet is smaller.
5 The cat is not on the filing cabinet, but in the in-tray by the desk where the two men are playing cards.
6 It's a lorry that is parked outside, not a bus.
7 The woman has fair hair.
8 There is no cake on the woman's desk.
9 The two men have dark hair.
10 The office boy is reading the paper, not playing cards.

(continued on page 92)

28 Prepositions of place *(continued)*

D Work in pairs. You each have a picture. The pictures are similar, but there are ten differences. By asking questions about where things are in the pictures, find out what the differences are. Don't show your picture to your partner.

Picture 1

D Work in pairs. You each have a picture. The pictures are similar, but there are ten differences. By asking questions about where things are in the pictures, find out what the differences are. Don't show your picture to your partner.

Picture 2

From *Instant Lessons 1 Elementary* edited by Peter Watcyn-Jones © Penguin Books 2000

Teacher's notes

Homework

Activity E Set this exercise for homework. Let them exchange their answers when they bring the work back.

Key

E 1 on 2 in 3 behind 4 under/on 5 above 6 in
7 opposite 8 next to 9 near 10 near 11 in 12 on

28 Prepositions of place (continued)

E In the story below, choose the correct preposition: *above, behind, in, near, next to, on, opposite, under*.

Nick was standing (1)_____ the beach when he saw Joe sitting (2)_____ the small boat. The beach was empty. Now was his chance. He went (3)_____ a large rock and changed his clothes. He put the clothes (4)_____ some stones at the back of the beach.

Then he ran to the sea, shouting and waving to Joe. Soon he was swimming out to the boat. He was laughing and shouting to Joe. Joe looked pleased to see him. It was very quiet, until he heard the noise of a helicopter. He looked up and saw the helicopter flying (5)_____ them. It didn't move, but just circled there.

He reached the boat and Joe helped him to climb (6)_____.

'Got any fish?'

'No. Nothing today.'

'That helicopter's making a lot of noise. I wish it would go away.'

'Yes. It's not good for the fish.'

At first, they sat (7)_____ each other at different ends of the boat. Then Nick moved to sit (8)_____ Joe.

'Careful. Don't rock the boat!'

'We'll have to swim!'

'I can't swim,' said Joe.

Nick smiled quietly. He knew that. Then Nick saw another boat. At the moment, it wasn't (9)_____ them. But he must kill Joe quickly before the other boat came (10)_____. And there was the helicopter.

'Let me have the fishing line. I'll catch some fish.'

'Hey! Careful. You'll have me (11)_____ the water,' Joe said as Nick took the fishing line from him. Then Nick jumped up and the boat rocked again.

'Give it to me. Give me the line,' he shouted.

The boat rocked again and they both fell into the water.

'Help!' Joe was shouting as Nick pulled himself into the boat. Nick started the engine and then took the boat to the beach. He jumped out of the boat and ran. He was shouting: 'Help! Help! My friend. He fell out of the boat. He can't swim. Help!'

But there was nobody (12)_____ the beach. Joe was dead.

From *Instant Lessons 1 Elementary* edited by Peter Watcyn-Jones © Penguin Books 2000

Teacher's notes

29 Adverbs

Aim	To introduce adverbs of manner: to show how they are formed from adjectives and their position in an unmarked sentence.
Preparation	Activity A: Copy and cut up the cards on page 95 – one set per group. Activities B and C: Copy the handout on page 95 – one copy per student.

Introduction (5 minutes)

Introduce the topic by talking about some of the students. For example: *I saw Charlotte coming to school today. She was very quick. Yes, Charlotte walks quickly.*
Write the last part on the board.
Anna took a long time to do that exercise. She's a slow worker. She works slowly.
Again, write the last part on the board.
It is always easy to mark William's work. He has beautiful writing. He writes beautifully.
Write the last part on the board and then underline the *-ly* at the end of each adverb. Then ask individual students about themselves. For example: *How do you work? Are you a quick runner?* etc. When they reply, encourage them to give the answer in the form which requires the adverb.

Presentation (15 minutes)

Explain you are talking about adverbs which tell you how something is done. Adjectives answer the question *What kind of ...?*
For example: *What kind of worker is Charlotte? She is a quick worker. How does she work? She works quickly.*
Point out on the board that adjectives come before nouns, but adverbs come after verbs and at the end of the sentence. For example:
Chris is a beautiful singer. Chris sings beautifully. Chris sang that song beautifully.
Write these adjectives on the board: *quick, beautiful, happy, ugly, soft, wonderful, crazy, lovely, good, hard, fast*. Then ask the students if they know what the adverb derived from each one is: *quickly, beautifully, happily, in an ugly way, softly, wonderfully, crazily, in a lovely way, well, hard, fast*.
Tell the students that the general rule is to add *-ly* to the adjective, but:

1 When the adjective ends in *y*, e.g. *happy, easy*, you change the *y* to *i* and then add *-ly*.
2 When the adjective ends in *-ly*, e.g. *lively, ugly*, you must make a phrase: *in a lively way, in an ugly way*.
3 There are some exceptions. Look at these:
   He's a good worker.   He works well.
   She's a fast runner.   She runs fast.
   They're hard workers.   They work hard.

Practice (20 minutes)

Activity A The students play the card game in groups. Give each group a set of the cards. The cards are dealt out among the group. To start the game, a student puts down an adjective card. The student with the equivalent adverb puts down that card followed by a new adjective card. If a student has both the adjective and adverb in his/her hand, he/she puts them both down at the beginning of the game. The game continues until one student has used all his/her cards.

Activity B In pairs, the students ask each other the questions. The questions use the adjective form, but the answers must use the adverb form. (If you plan to use the answers to the questionnaire as the basis for homework, remember to ask students to note down their partner's answers.)

Conclusion (10 minutes)

Activity C The students work individually on the exercise. Check orally.

Homework

The students write a profile based on the answers they had to the questionnaire. They must use the adverb form. For example: *Laura works hard. She drives badly*, etc.

Key

C   1   He drives dangerously.
    2   Harry works fast.
    3   Joanna writes well.
    4   It's snowing heavily now.
    5   Phil eats noisily.
    6   Annie teaches in a lively way.
    7   Martin cooks badly.
    8   He talks loudly.
    9   Steve and Joshua play tennis cleverly.
   10   Mark paints beautifully.

29 Adverbs

A

quick	slow	fast	good
beautiful	quickly	slowly	fast
well	beautifully	happy	ugly
bad	clever	hard	happily
in an ugly way	badly	cleverly	hard
easy	lively	stupid	quiet
careful	easily	in a lively way	stupidly
quietly	carefully	sad	lovely
crazy	brave	cruel	sadly
in a lovely way	crazily	bravely	cruelly

B Ask your partner these questions. When you give your answers, you must use the adverb form. For example:
Are you a slow runner?
Yes, I run slowly. OR
No, I don't run slowly.

1. Are you a hard worker?
2. Are you a good driver?
3. Are you a beautiful singer?
4. Are you a bad dancer?
5. Are you a quick learner?
6. Are you a fast runner?
7. Are you a careful driver?
8. Are you a slow worker?
9. Are you a quiet speaker?
10. Are you a good cook?

C Rewrite these sentences using the adverb form. For example:
John's a good driver.
John drives well.
That dog has a loud bark.
That dog barks loudly.

1. He's a dangerous driver.
2. Harry's a fast worker.
3. Joanna is a good writer.
4. The snow is heavy now.
5. Phil is a noisy eater.
6. Annie is a lively teacher.
7. Martin is a bad cook.
8. He's a loud talker.
9. Steve and Joshua are clever tennis players.
10. Mark is a beautiful painter.

From *Instant Lessons 1 Elementary* edited by Peter Watcyn-Jones © Penguin Books 2000

Teacher's notes

30 Demonstratives and possessives

Aim:	To show the use of demonstratives (*this*, *that*, *these*, *those*), the use of possessive pronouns (*mine*, *yours*, *his*, *hers*, *ours*, *theirs*) and to give students practice in using them.
Preparation:	Copy the handouts on pages 97 and 99 – one copy per student.

Introduction *(5 minutes)*

First take some books from the students. Keep some by you and place others in different parts of the room. Then, taking a book near you, ask: *Whose is this book?* Write the question on the board.
Then point to a book across the room and ask: *Whose is that book?*
Then, holding up two or three books: *Whose are these books?*
Then point to several books: *Whose are those books?*
Always write the questions on the board. Then get some students to come up to the front and repeat the procedure.

Presentation *(15 minutes)*

Explain the difference between *this/that* and *these/those* on the board:

	when it's here	when it's over there
singular	this	that
plural	these	those

Then get different objects from the students: pens, books, pencils, rulers, watches, rings, etc. Hold up your own watch and ask: *Whose is this watch?* Give the answer: *It's mine.* Write the answer on the board.
Then hold up an object and ask: *Who does this belong to?* Elicit from the owner: *It's mine.*
Then say to the rest of the class: *This belongs to ... It's hers/his.* Write this on the board.
Then hold up another object and ask a student (one you know is not the owner): *Is this ... yours?*
Repeat this procedure, making sure you bring in all the different forms of question. Then hand back the objects randomly. When students comment that they have not got their own things back, get them to ask each other who the object they have belongs to.

Practice *(20 minutes)*

Activity A Students do the exercise individually. Check orally.

(continued on page 98)

Key

A 1 this   2 that   3 that   4 This   5 that   6 these
   7 those   8 that   9 that   10 that   11 this   12 that
   13 Those   14 that   15 those   16 that   17 that
   18 Those   19 those   20 those

(continued on page 98)

30 Demonstratives and possessives

A Dave and Gerry are students moving into a new flat. Joe is helping Dave arrange the furniture and things.

Look at the picture and complete the text with *this*, *that*, *these* or *those*.

Now, Joe. Put (1) _____ armchair next to (2) _____ table in the corner over there. Then put (3) _____ chair, the one in the middle of the room, by the window. (4) _____ cupboard goes against (5) _____ wall by the window. Now (6) _____ books go on (7) _____ shelves by (8) _____ door. Yes, (9) _____ door to the kitchen. Can you move (10) _____ table to the window and then put (11) _____ chair here in front of it. Careful with (12) _____ vase. It's mine. (13) _____ old magazines on the floor over there belong to Gerry. He's saving them. For the moment, put them on (14) _____ cupboard that you've moved to the window. And (15) _____ dishes on (16) _____ box go into the kitchen. What's in (17) _____ box, by the way? Books? Whose books? Oh, I know. (18) _____ books you've put on the shelves are mine. And (19) _____ books in the box belong to Gerry. I'm getting tired. Give me (20) _____ two cups on the table. I'll make some tea.

From *Instant Lessons 1 Elementary* edited by Peter Watcyn-Jones © Penguin Books 2000

Teacher's notes

Activity B The students work in pairs to match the sentences. Make this a competitive exercise to see which pair finishes first. Check orally.

Conclusion *(10 minutes)*

Activity C The students work individually. Check orally.

Key

B 1 a/d/f   2 a/d   3 j   4 h   5 b   6 i
   7 a/d/f   8 g   9 c   10 e

C 1 That, mine   2 That, theirs   3 Those, hers
   4 This, mine   5 That, his   6 these, theirs   7 that, yours
   8 this, mine   9 these, mine   10 that, his

30 Demonstratives and possessives
(continued)

B Match a sentence in column 1 with one in column 2. There may be more than one possible match, but you can use each item in column 2 once only.

1	2
1 This isn't Sarah's bicycle.	a Is it yours?
2 Give me that picture.	b But it isn't theirs.
3 I like these wine glasses.	c But mine were bad.
4 Would you like that book?	d It's mine.
5 John and Rita like that red car.	e Give him yours.
6 Is this your ball?	f Hers is red.
7 This isn't Jane's coat.	g No, it doesn't. It's mine.
8 That watch belongs to Matt.	h Then take it. It's yours.
9 Dave's exam results were good.	i No, it's hers.
10 Andy needs a bicycle.	j Yes, they are nice. They're his.

C Complete the sentences by putting in the correct word in the gaps. Choose from: *this, that, these, those, mine, yours, his, hers, ours, theirs*.

1 .... book there belongs to me. It's ....
2 .... dog in the park over there belongs to Matt and Sue. It's ....
3 .... parrots in the cage there belong to Sarah. They're ....
4 .... car that I'm sitting in belongs to me. It's ....
5 .... watch on the table there was a present to Andy. It's ....
6 Mr and Mrs Davis bought .... flowers in the vase here on the table. They're ....
7 I bought .... painting there for you. It's ....
8 Did Dave sell .... table here to you? Yes, it's ....
9 I found .... wooden figures here in Poland. Now they're ....
10 Is .... red car there Stephen's? Yes, it's ....

Vocabulary: Lessons 31–40

31 Clothes

Aim	To teach some basic clothing vocabulary, including a few accessories.
Preparation	Copy the handouts on pages 101 and 103 – one copy per pair. Cut in half the handout on page 103.
(Optional)	Wear something unusual or outrageous to the lesson.

Introduction *(5 minutes)*

Point to an item of clothing you are wearing (particularly something you're wearing specially for the lesson) and tell the class that it's a present you got from your wife/husband/brother. Ask them what they think of it? (You'll find out how diplomatic your students are!) Tell them that today they're going to learn the names for different clothes.

Presentation *(20 minutes)*

Activity A Divide the class into pairs. Give each pair a copy of the handout. Tell them to see how many items of clothing they already know by writing the correct numbers next to the words. Allow 15 minutes. Check orally, paying particular attention to the words that were new. For the next 5 minutes, get the students to take turns at testing each other. One student (the one being tested) covers up the words while his/her partner asks him/her: *What's number 8?* etc.

(continued on page 102)

Key

A *For him*: baseball cap 18, belt 16, jacket 2, jeans 3, mac 9, pendant 12, shirt 13, shoes 8, suit 7, sunglasses 6, tie 15, trousers 10, T-shirt 14, umbrella 4, underpants 11, vest 1, waistcoat 17, wallet 5
For her: blouse 3, boots 11, bra 1, coat 13, dress 2, earrings 10, glasses 8, handbag 9, hat 6, jumper 16, knickers 7, necklace 14, purse 12, skirt 15, socks 4, tights 17, trainers 5

(continued on page 102)

Teacher's notes

31 Clothes

A Write the numbers 1–18 next to the correct word(s).

For him

baseball cap ☐   belt ☐   jacket ☐   jeans ☐
mac ☐   pendant ☐   shirt ☐   shoes ☐
suit ☐
sunglasses ☐
tie ☐
trousers ☐
T-shirt ☐
umbrella ☐
underpants ☐
vest ☐
waistcoat ☐
wallet ☐

Write the numbers 1–17 next to the correct word(s).

For her

blouse ☐   boots ☐   bra ☐   coat ☐
dress ☐   earrings ☐   glasses ☐   handbag ☐
hat ☐
jumper ☐
knickers ☐
necklace ☐
purse ☐
skirt ☐
socks ☐
tights ☐
trainers ☐

From *Instant Lessons 1 Elementary* edited by Peter Watcyn-Jones © Penguin Books 2000

Teacher's notes

Practice (20 minutes)

Activity B This is a pairwork exercise where students have to try to find the differences between two drawings showing three people. Give one student in each pair picture 1, and the other picture 2. Get them to face each other and to hide their papers. Explain that they now take it in turns to ask and answer questions in order to find the differences between their drawings. Give some examples of question types, then write them on the board. For example:
Is the woman on the left wearing (a skirt)?
What colour are the man's (shoes)?
Is the woman on the right holding (an umbrella)?
etc.
Tell them to put a circle around any differences they find. Also teach the words *stripy* and *checked*.
Halfway through the activity you can tell them that there are ten differences altogether. At the end of the activity, they check their drawings to make sure they have found everything.

Conclusion (5 minutes)

Go back to Activity A. Ask them which clothes are often worn by both men and women. Also find out which clothes the students wear most often.

Homework

The students can write a short paragraph describing how they are usually dressed when they go out at the weekend. Alternatively, you can ask them to write a paragraph suggesting what clothes they would like to see you in.

Key

B *Differences in picture 2:*
1 The woman on the left isn't wearing glasses.
2 Her boots are black, not white.
3 The man isn't wearing a tie.
4 He's wearing jeans, not trousers.
5 He's wearing trainers, not shoes.
6 He's got an earring.
7 He hasn't got an umbrella.
8 The woman on the right is wearing a coat, not a mac.
9 Her dress is black, not stripy.
10 Her shoes are black, not white.

31 Clothes (continued)

B Find the differences.

Picture 1

B Find the differences.

Picture 2

From *Instant Lessons 1 Elementary* edited by Peter Watcyn-Jones © Penguin Books 2000

Teacher's notes

32 Foot + ball = football

Aim	To teach the students some common compound nouns.
Preparation	Copy handouts on pages 105 and 107 – one copy per student. Cut up the words in Activity B.

Introduction *(5 minutes)*

Draw the following on the board:

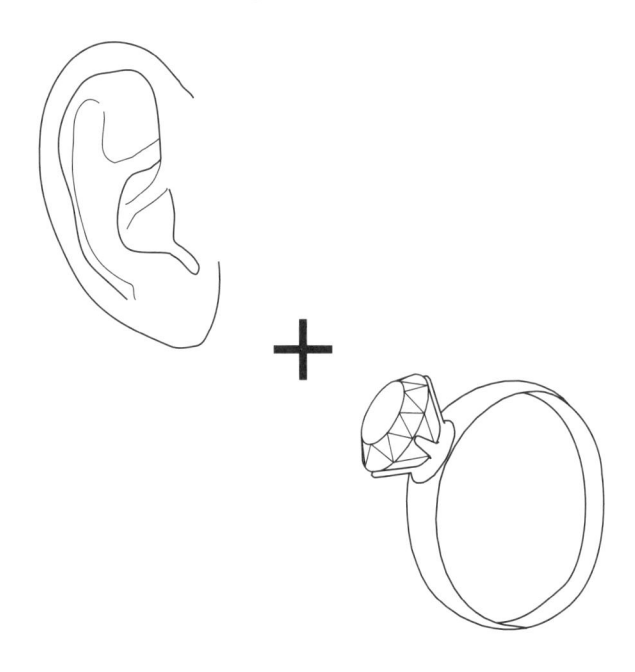

Ask the students if they can guess what the word is from the drawing. (The answer is *earring*.) Tell them it is common in English to put two words together to form a completely new word. Give them another example, namely *football*. (Draw it if you can!) Ask the students for any other examples they know.

Presentation *(20 minutes)*

Activity A Divide the class into pairs. Give each student a copy of the handout. Explain that they have to use the clues to match words from column 1 with words from column 2 to make ten completely new words. Some words in the columns will not be used.

Practice *(15 minutes)*

Activity B Students work alone at first. Give each student one of the words on page 105 plus a copy of the blank drawing sheet on page 107. Before they start, make sure they understand the meaning of the word they are going to draw. Tell them to try to represent the word on the blank sheet of paper by drawing two pictures, one for the first part of the word and one for the second. Allow approximately 5 minutes.
When everyone is ready, they now walk around the class talking to as many people as possible. They take it in turns to try and guess each other's words.
At the end of the activity, get one or two volunteers to draw their word on the board.

(continued on page 106)

Key

A 1 waistcoat   2 keyboard   3 postcard   4 toothbrush
   5 bathroom   6 birthday   7 armchair   8 suitcase
   9 handbag   10 lighthouse

(continued on page 106)

32 Foot + ball = football

A Match words from column 1 with words from column 2 to make compound words.

1 It's something people wear – usually men. _____

2 A musical instrument. It's like a piano. _____

3 You can write this when you're on holiday. _____

4 You use it to keep your teeth clean. _____

5 Where you have a shower. _____

6 Everybody has one of these once a year. _____

7 You can sit in it. _____

8 You put clothes in this when you go on holiday. _____

9 Women keep their money and makeup in this. _____

10 A tall building near the sea. It helps boats. _____

column 1	column 2
arm	bag
bath	ball
birth	board
boy	brush
hand	card
key	case
lamp	chair
light	coat
post	day
suit	house
tooth	room
waist	table

B Words

bedroom	butterfly	nightdress	cowboy
penknife	screwdriver	schoolgirl	farmhouse
headphones	lipstick	seatbelt	sunglasses
lamppost	housewife	rainbow	moonlight
timetable	basketball	cupboard	postman

From *Instant Lessons 1 Elementary* edited by Peter Watcyn-Jones © Penguin Books 2000

Teacher's notes

Conclusion *(10 minutes)*

Activity C This is a quick check to see if the students have remembered some of the words practised in the lesson. They can work in pairs. Check orally.

Homework

Ask the students to draw and make up gapped sentences for the following compound nouns: *bookcase, bagpipes* and *haircut*.

Key

C 1 football 2 birthday 3 waistcoat 4 cowboy
   5 bathroom 6 seatbelt 7 postcard 8 postman
   9 armchair 10 cupboard

32 Foot + ball = football (continued)

B Drawings

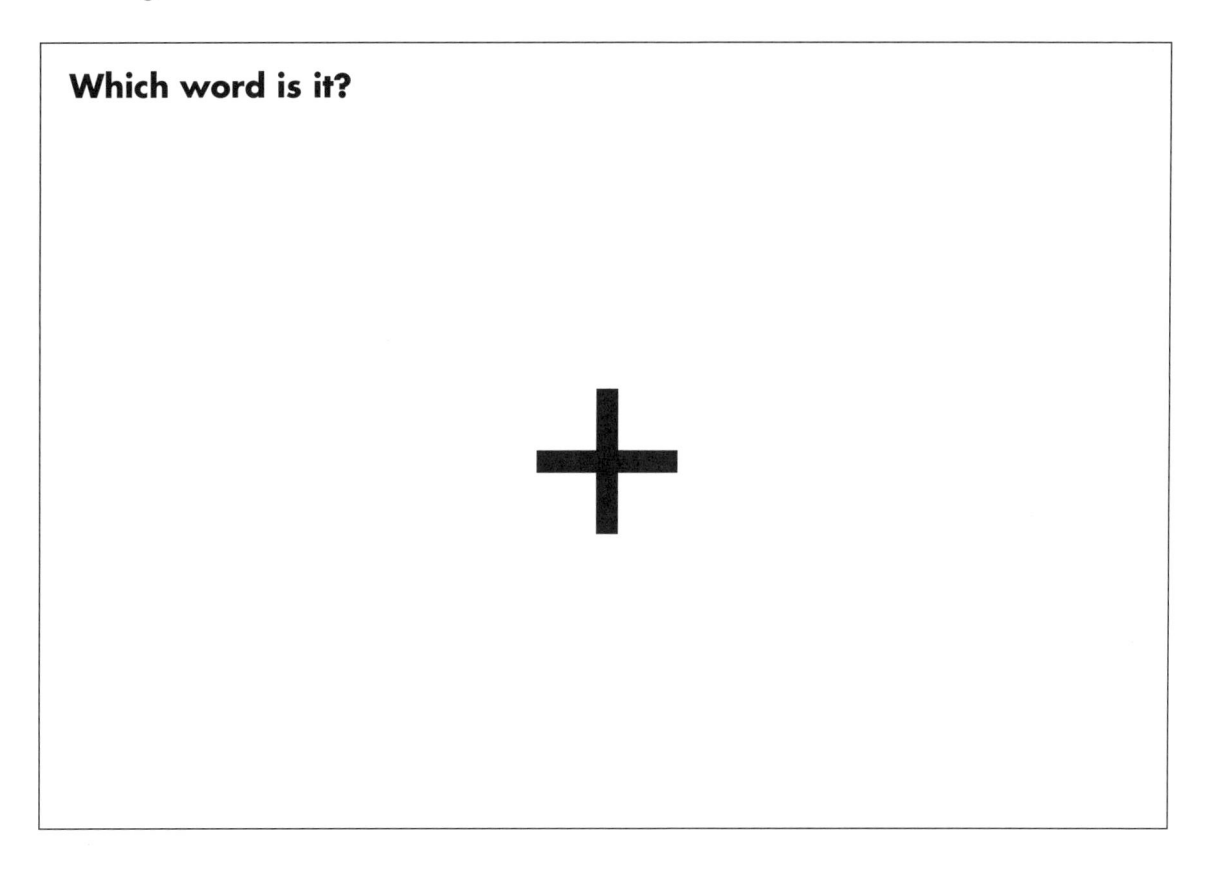

Which word is it?

➕

C Fill in the missing words. To help you, the first and last letters of each word are given.

1 'What's your favourite sport?'

   'F_____l, of course.'

2 I got this camera from my parents for my b_____y.

3 Shall I buy a suit with or without a w_____t?

4 John Wayne often played a c_____y in films.

5 'Where's Paula?'

   'She's in the b_____m washing her hair.'

6 When you travel by car you should always wear a s_____t.

7 Don't forget to send me a p_____d from Spain!

8 'Is there a letter for me?' 'I don't know. The p_____n hasn't come yet.'

9 Sit down in that a_____r over there.

10 'Where are the plates and glasses?'

   'In the c_____d in the kitchen.'

From *Instant Lessons 1 Elementary* edited by Peter Watcyn-Jones © Penguin Books 2000

Teacher's notes

33 The living room

Aim	To teach the most common items of furniture and fittings found in the living room.
Preparation	Copy the handouts on pages 109 and 111 – one copy per student.

Introduction (5 minutes)

Introduce the subject by telling the students that you feel a bit tired today because you decided to move all the furniture around in your living room last night, mainly because your new sofa had arrived. (Describe the sofa if you like.) Ask the students what other pieces of furniture can be found in the living room. Write these up on the board.

Presentation (20 minutes)

Activity A Give students the handout. Allow a maximum of 10 minutes. Check orally, paying special attention to pronunciation. Now let the students work in pairs. One student covers the words while the other student tests him/her by asking: *What's number 1?* etc. When they have done it once, they change roles and do it again.

Practice (15 minutes)

Activity B Give students a copy of the picture. Tell them to look carefully at the drawing for 5 minutes, without writing anything down. Tell them to turn their papers over and hand out the list of questions. They work in pairs. Allow 5 minutes, then let them check by referring to the picture again.

(continued on page 110)

Key

A armchair 19, bookcase 24, carpet 20, ceiling 4, coffee table 22, curtains 2, cushion 18, fireplace 23, lamp 16, light switch 3, mirror 13, painting 7, plant 8, power point 11, radiator 12, side table 17, sofa 15, speakers 5, stereo 6, TV 9, vase 21, video 10 wallpaper 14, window 1

B 1 Yes 2 Two 3 More than 3 4 No 5 Yes 6 No
7 Three 8 No 9 No 10 Yes

(continued on page 110)

33 The living room

A Write the numbers (1–24) next to the correct words.

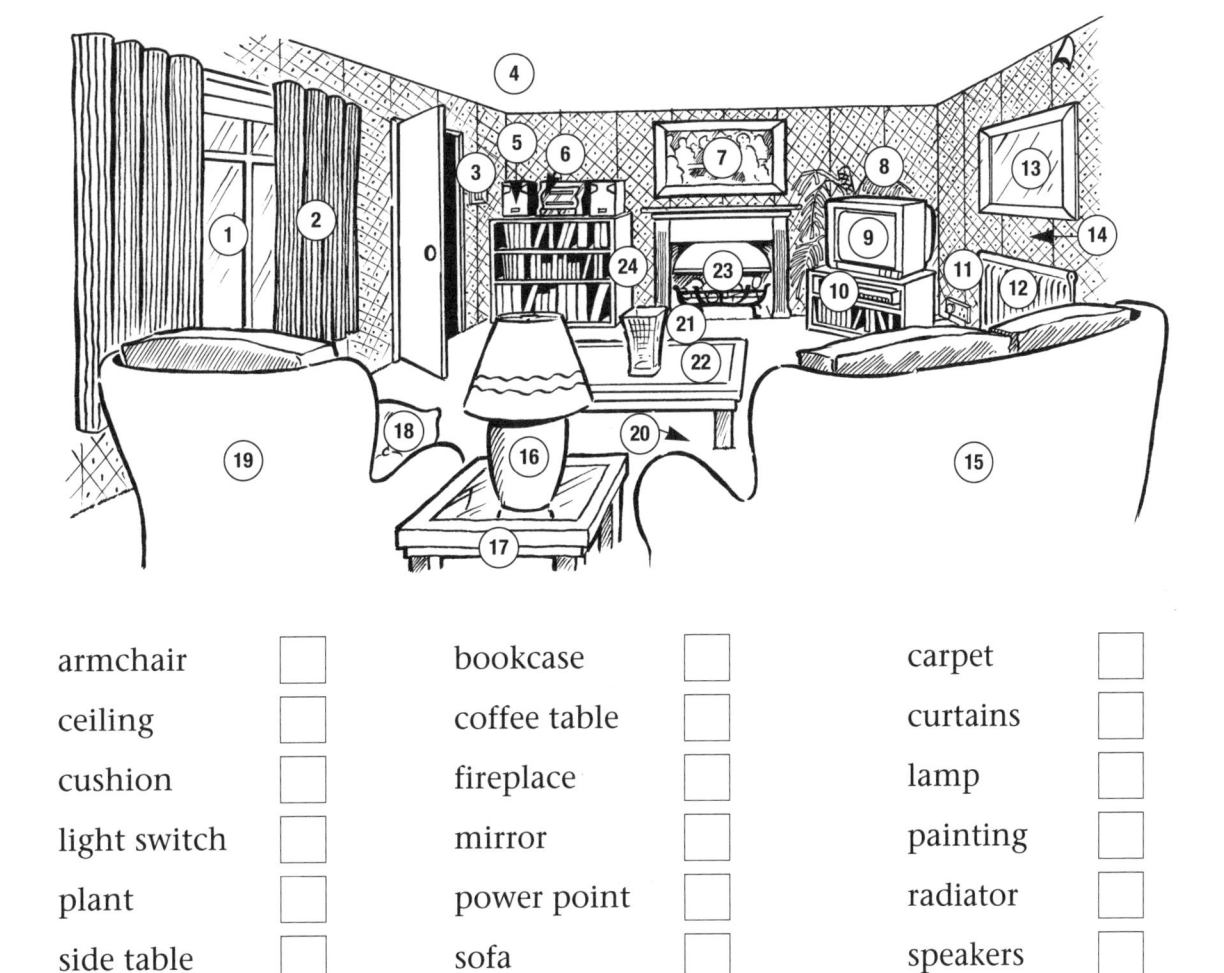

armchair	☐	bookcase	☐	carpet	☐
ceiling	☐	coffee table	☐	curtains	☐
cushion	☐	fireplace	☐	lamp	☐
light switch	☐	mirror	☐	painting	☐
plant	☐	power point	☐	radiator	☐
side table	☐	sofa	☐	speakers	☐
stereo	☐	TV	☐	vase	☐
video	☐	wallpaper	☐	window	☐

B Look at this drawing for five minutes.

From *Instant Lessons 1 Elementary* edited by Peter Watcyn-Jones © Penguin Books 2000

Teacher's notes

Conclusion (10 minutes)

Activity C This is a check to see if the students have remembered the words practised in the lesson. They can work in pairs. Check orally.

Homework

The students draw a plan of their living room, seen from above. They should label the furniture, etc., including its colour.

Key

C 1 curtains   2 ceiling   3 armchair   4 carpet
   5 speakers   6 bookcase   7 wallpaper   8 coffee table
   9 sofa   10 plant

33 The living room (continued)

B Now read the questions and circle the correct answers.

1 Are there flowers in the vase?	Yes	No
2 How many power points are there in the room?	1 2 3	
3 How many paintings are there?	Fewer than 3	
	More than 3	
4 Is the lamp next to the armchair?	Yes	No
5 Is the TV on?	Yes	No
6 Is the vase on the coffee table?	Yes	No
7 How many cushions are there?	1 2 3	
8 Is there a video in the room?	Yes	No
9 Are the curtains stripy?	Yes	No
10 Is the mirror next to the bookcase?	Yes	No

C Which words are missing? See if you can work it out.

1 Do you like the new green _____ in the window? (*austicrn*)

2 This room has a very high _____. (*licegin*)

3 This _____ is very comfortable. (*rachmari*)

4 That's a nice _____ on the floor! (*actper*)

5 Where shall I put the _____? Where do you sit when you listen to music? (*raspskee*)

6 What a lot of interesting things in your _____! (*cokesboa*)

7 I hate yellow _____! (*rappelawl*)

8 The magazine was on the _____. (*ocfefe elatb*)

9 At least three people can sit in this _____. (*afos*)

10 There was a large green _____ in the corner of the room. (*tapln*)

Teacher's notes

34 Countries and nationalities

Aim	To teach the names of some common countries and nationalities.
Preparation	Copy the handout on page 113 – one copy per student.
(Optional)	Take in some magazine photos of people from different countries.

Introduction (5 minutes)

Introduce the subject by saying to the students that foreigners often call people living in Britain or the UK *English* and think that everyone lives in *England*. But that's not really true. Draw a rough map of the UK and explain that the UK is made up of four countries, not one. See if the students know the other countries, namely Scotland, Wales and Northern Ireland. Write them on the map. Then write the following on the board:

I live in ... England   I'm ... English
Scotland
Wales
Northern Ireland

Elicit the missing nationalities (*Scottish, Welsh* and *Northern Irish*). Point out that people from all these countries are also *British*. Practise saying the names of the countries chorally. Finally, ask one or two students about themselves, for example: *What about you, Kurt? Where do you live? What nationality are you?* etc.

Alternative introduction Hold up the photographs you have brought with you one by one and ask the class if they can guess what nationality the person is. Why did they think the person was (Swedish)? Was it the clothes, skin/hair colour, etc.? Then go on to the above table about the four nationalities in the UK.

Presentation (15 minutes)

Activity A Give students the handout. Let them work in pairs to fill it in. When they have finished, write the following on the board:
A: *Are you **Swedish**?*
B: *No, I'm **French**. I come from **France**.*
Get them to practise similar dialogues in pairs, choosing other nationalities from the ones in the table.

Practice (20 minutes)

Activity B This is a crossword dictation. The students can either work alone or in pairs. Give out copies of the crossword and tell the students you are going to read out clues to help them to fill in the crossword. All the answers are either a country or a nationality. Read out the following clues, allowing time for them to fill in the answers. (You can read each clue twice.)

Let's start with 8 Across: Honda, Yamaha and Canon are all __(bleep!)__ companies.
Next, 9 Down: Elvis Presley was a famous __(bleep!)__ pop singer.
10 Across: Flamenco is a traditional dance in this country.
2 Down: You can see kangaroos and koalas in this country.
6 Down: Juventus is a famous __(bleep!)__ football team.
11 Across: This is a small country with lots of banks and lots of mountains. It has a lake called Lake Geneva.
11 Down: Abba was a famous __(bleep!)__ pop group.
14 Across: There are more __(bleep!)__ people in the world than any other nationality.
5 Across: Vodka is a popular __(bleep!)__ drink.
3 Down: Istanbul is the biggest city in this country.
4 Across: The most famous __(bleep!)__ city is Amsterdam.
1 Across: The samba is a typical __(bleep!)__ dance.
13 Across: Beethoven and Bach were famous __(bleep!)__ composers.
7 Down: The capital of this country is Brussels.
Finally, 12 Down: People in this country eat a lot of curry.

Check orally.

Conclusion (10 minutes)

Activity C This is a fun activity. The students complete the sentences then compare their answers with a partner.

Homework

The students can write a short paragraph about the country they live in.

Key

A American, Australia, Belgian, Brazilian, Canada, China, Dutch, France, Germany, Greek, India, Italian, Japanese, Portugal, Russia, Saudi Arabian, Spanish, Swedish, Switzerland, Turkish

B Across: 1 Brazilian 4 Dutch 5 Russian 8 Japanese 10 Spain 11 Switzerland 13 German 14 Chinese
Down: 2 Australia 3 Turkey 6 Italian 7 Belgium 9 American 11 Swedish 12 India

34 Countries and nationalities

A Complete the table.

I live in ...	I'm ...	I live in ...	I'm ...
the USA			Indian
	Australian	Italy	
Belgium		Japan	
Brazil			Portuguese
	Canadian		Russian
	Chinese	Saudi Arabia	
The Netherlands		Spain	
	French	Sweden	
	German		Swiss
Greece		Turkey	

B

C Complete the sentences in your own words.

1 The best cars come from _____.

2 They make the best food in _____.

3 The best football players come from _____.

4 The best climate is in _____.

5 _____ people are the friendliest.

6 _____ women are the most beautiful.

7 _____ men are the most romantic.

8 The best pop music comes from _____.

9 My favourite country for a holiday is _____.

10 If I could be another nationality, I'd like to be _____.

From *Instant Lessons 1 Elementary* edited by Peter Watcyn-Jones © Penguin Books 2000

Teacher's notes

35 What do they look like?

Aim	To teach useful words for describing people. It is assumed that the students will have done the lesson on clothes (Lesson 31) before doing this lesson.
Preparation	Copy the handouts on pages 115 and 117 – one or two copies per student. Cut page 115 in half.

Introduction *(5 minutes)*

Introduce the subject by pretending that you have recently witnessed a crime, for example a car theft, and had to give the police a description of the man you saw steal the car. Explain that it was very difficult. (As you tell the next bit, write up all the key words on the board.) All you can remember was that he was quite *tall*, *slim* and had *long hair*. Oh yes, and he had a *moustache*. Ask the class for other words they know to describe people. Write them up on the board.

Presentation *(15 minutes)*

Activity A Give a copy to each student. Let them work in pairs. Check orally.

Practice *(25 minutes)*

Activity B This is a roleplay in pairs. Put the class into pairs and ask them to decide who will be Student 1 and who will be Student 2. Hand out the appropriate handouts. Explain that Student 1 is someone whose brother, sister or friend has gone missing and Student 2 is a police officer. Student 1 phones Student 2 to give a description of the missing person. Student 2 writes down all the details on the Missing Persons form. Allow a few minutes for them to prepare, then let the roleplay begin. When they have done it once they can change roles and do it again. (Give out new handouts.)

(continued on page 116)

Key

A 1 is fat 2 is well-built
   3 is slim 4 is skinny
   5 is about forty 6 is old
   7 is young 8 is about 160cm
   9 is short 10 is tall
   11 has a beard 12 has a moustache
   13 has blonde hair 14 has dark hair
   15 has curly hair 16 has long hair
   17 has short hair 18 is bald
   19 has freckles 20 wears glasses

35 What do they look like?

A Match the words and the drawings.

has a beard ☐	has a moustache ☐	has blonde hair ☐
has curly hair ☐	has dark hair ☐	has freckles ☐
has long hair ☐	has short hair ☐	is about 160cm ☐
is about forty ☐	is bald ☐	is fat ☐
is old ☐	is short ☐	is skinny ☐
is slim ☐	is tall ☐	is well-built ☐
is young ☐	wears glasses ☐	

build — age — height — hair/face

B Student 1

Imagine that someone you know (your brother, mother, friend, etc.) is missing. You phone the police station to report it. You will be asked questions about his/her:

• name • age • height • build • colour of eyes • hair (colour, style) •
other things (moustache, wears glasses, etc.) • clothes •
where last seen (at home, on the way to work, etc.)

When you have finished, change roles and do it again.

From *Instant Lessons 1 Elementary* edited by Peter Watcyn-Jones © Penguin Books 2000

Teacher's notes

Conclusion *(5 minutes)*

Each student writes a short description of himself/herself on a separate piece of paper, but must **not** include name or address. Take one or two at random and read them out loud. See if the rest of the class can guess who is being described.

Homework

The students can write a short description of one of the following:
My favourite relative
My best friend
My teacher

35 What do they look like? *(continued)*

B Student 2

You work at the Missing Persons department at the police station. Student 1 phones you to report a missing person. Ask him/her questions and fill in this form.

Missing Person

Name: ....

Address: ....

Age: ....

Height: ....

Build: ....

Colour of eyes: ....

Hair colour: ....

Hair style: ....

Anything else?: ....

Clothes worn: ....

Place last seen: ....

Before you start, work out what questions to ask. For example:

What's his/her name/address?

How old ...?

What's his/her build?

What colour is/are ...?

What style ...?

Anything else?

What was he/she wearing?

Where was he/she last seen?

When you have finished, change roles and do it again.

From *Instant Lessons 1 Elementary* edited by Peter Watcyn-Jones © Penguin Books 2000

Teacher's notes

36 Food

Aim	To teach some basic food vocabulary, plus food words encountered on a simple restaurant menu.
Preparation	Copy the handout on page 119 – one copy per student.

Introduction (5 minutes)

Introduce the subject by talking a little bit about food and the things you like eating. For example: *I love eating – especially bananas and ice cream. Bananas are my favourite fruit. Well, I like apples too. And I really like cooking. Last night, for example, I made spaghetti followed by apple pie and custard. What about you? What things do you like eating?*
Then write the following drill on the board:
A: *I like ...* (apples)
B: *Yes, so do I.*
or *Oh, I don't. But I like ...* (bananas)
Practise it with one or two students so they understand the pattern. Then let them practise in pairs, using any food words they already know.

Presentation 1 (15 minutes)

Activity A Give students a copy of the handout. Explain that they have to put six words in each group. Let them work in pairs. Check orally. (You may have to explain some of the meat words by drawing or miming the animals.)

Practice 1 (5 minutes)

This is a game for pairs. One student turns over his/her handout. The other student then says a word, for example banana. The first student answers as quickly as possible with one of the following: *It's a fruit / a vegetable / a drink / a type of meat / a type of fish or seafood.*
Write the possible responses on the board to help them. Demonstrate first with the whole class, then let the students practise. After about 2 minutes, tell them to change roles and do it again. Stop everyone after 5 minutes.

Presentation 2 (15 minutes)

Activity B Ask students to look at the simple menu. Go through it to make sure that the students understand each word. Also write on the board the following phrases, useful when ordering in a restaurant:
What would you like ...   to start with?
*   for the main course?*
*   for dessert?*
*   to drink?*
I'd like ...
Could I have the bill, please?
Go through the above chorally. Then demonstrate with one or two students. (You play the waiter/waitress.)

Practice 2 (10 minutes)

The students now work in pairs to act out the roleplay. They take it in turns to be the customer and the waiter/waitress.

Conclusion (5 minutes)

Divide the class into groups of four. Tell them to write the numbers 1–6 on a piece of paper. One person will write for the whole group. Read out the following, allowing students time to write down their answers.
1 Name a fruit beginning with the letter g.
2 Name a vegetable beginning with the letter c.
3 Name a fish beginning with the letter s.
4 Name a drink beginning with the letter w.
5 Name another fruit beginning with the letter m.
6 Name another vegetable beginning with the letter o.
Check orally. Give 1 point for each correct answer. How many teams got 6 points?

Homework

The students use a dictionary to find out the names of three more fruits, vegetables and fish or seafood. (You can compare words in the next lesson.)

Key

A fruits: apple, banana, grapes, melon, orange, pear
   vegetables: cabbage, carrot, cauliflower, onion, peas, potatoes
   meat: beef, chicken, ham, lamb, pork, veal
   fish and seafood: cod, crab, lobster, mussels, prawns, salmon
   drinks: beer, coffee, Coke, tea, water, wine
Conclusion
Although you are really expecting answers based on the words learnt during the lesson, allow other words the students may know.
1 grapes   2 cabbage/carrot/cauliflower   3 salmon
4 water/wine   5 melon   6 onion

36 Food

A Put the words in the correct groups. The first word in each group has already been done.

~~apple~~ banana ~~beef~~ ~~beer~~ cabbage carrot cauliflower chicken ~~cod~~ coffee Coke crab grapes ham lamb lobster melon mussels onion orange pear peas pork potatoes prawns salmon tea veal water wine

fruits	apple					
vegetables	cabbage					
meat	beef					
fish/seafood	cod					
drinks	beer					

B

The Gateway Restaurant
3-course meal £15 per person (drinks not included)

Starters
onion soup   fresh melon
prawn cocktail   smoked salmon

Main courses
spaghetti   roast beef
roast lamb   roast chicken
fresh cod

Vegetables
potatoes   French fries
peas   cauliflower
carrots   rice

Desserts
ice cream (chocolate, vanilla, strawberry)
cheese and biscuits
apple pie and custard
chocolate gateau

ssssssssssssssssssssssss

To drink (per glass)
soft drinks £1.50
(Coke, orange juice)
beer £2.50
mineral water £1.50
wine (red, white) £3

From *Instant Lessons 1 Elementary* edited by Peter Watcyn-Jones © Penguin Books 2000

Teacher's notes

37 Useful adjectives

Aim	To teach some common adjectives, including opposites and superlatives.
Preparation	Copy the handout on page 121 – one copy per student or pair.

Introduction (5 minutes)

Introduce the subject by writing the following on the board:
nouns: a chair, a knife, a mountain, a soldier, a pop singer
adjectives: high, famous, comfortable, brave, sharp
Tell the students to work in pairs and to try to match up the nouns with the adjectives. Check orally and explain any new words. Tell the students that in today's lesson you're going to be looking at adjectives.

Presentation (15 minutes)

Activity A Students work in pairs. Give each pair a copy of the handout. Do the first one orally with the whole class, then let them complete the rest of the exercise in pairs. Check orally and explain any new words. Ask for further examples of things that can be *ugly, dark, clean, open*, etc.
If there is time, the students can test each other. One student reads out an adjective from box 1 while his/her partner gives the correct opposite from the adjectives in box 2.

Practice (15 minutes)

Activity B This exercise uses adjectives from the introduction and Activity A, plus some new ones. The students can either work individually or in pairs. Check orally.

Conclusion (15 minutes)

Activity C This is a much freer activity based on the adjectives learnt during the lesson. Students work alone and complete the sentences in their own words. When they have finished, they find a partner and compare answers. If there is time, ask individual students to read out one of their sentences.

Homework

Write the following on the board. Tell the students that they have to try to name something or someone that is:
difficult   fat   light   weak   happy   nice   sweet   famous   round   modern

Key

Introduction
 a chair: comfortable
 a knife: sharp
 a mountain: high
 a soldier: brave
 a pop singer: famous

A 1 i 2 o 3 e 4 m 5 j 6 p 7 r 8 a 9 f 10 n 11 b
   12 k 13 g 14 c 15 q 16 l 17 d 18 h
B 1 funny 2 modern 3 thirsty 4 blunt 5 late 6 round
   7 wide 8 brave 9 rich 10 tired 11 empty 12 wet
   13 hungry 14 light 15 sweet 16 expensive

37 Useful adjectives

A Match each adjective from box 1 with the correct opposite from box 2. Write your answers in the boxes below.

box 1		
1 beautiful	7 fat	13 old
2 big	8 full	14 open
3 cheap	9 happy	15 strong
4 clean	10 high	16 tall
5 easy	11 hot	17 wet
6 fast	12 light	18 young

box 2		
a empty	g new	m dirty
b cold	h old	n low
c closed	i ugly	o small
d dry	j difficult	p slow
e expensive	k dark	q weak
f sad	l short	r thin

1	2	3	4	5	6	7	8	9	10	11	12	13	14	15	16	17	18

B Fill in the missing adjectives in the sentences below. Choose from the following. Use each adjective once only.

blunt brave empty expensive funny hungry late light modern rich round sweet thirsty tired wet wide

1 I think Charlie Chaplin films are very _____.
2 All my favourite buildings are _____ . They were built in the last ten years.
3 He needs a drink. He's _____.
4 A knife can be sharp or _____.
5 The train is _____ again!
6 A football is _____.
7 This river is very _____.
8 A police officer is usually _____.
9 A millionaire is _____.
10 I'm _____. I think I'll go to bed.
11 There's nothing in the box. It's _____.
12 Is it raining? This umbrella is _____.
13 She wants something to eat. She's _____.
14 A feather is _____.
15 Sugar is _____.
16 A diamond ring is usually _____.

C Complete the following sentences in your own words. (Write your answers on a separate piece of paper.)

1 The most beautiful woman in the world is ...
2 The hottest country I have ever visited is ...
3 You are fat when you weigh over ... (say how many kilos)
4 The fastest I have ever driven/travelled (choose) in a car is ... (say how many kilometres per hour)
5 You are old when you are over ... (say what age)
6 I always feel happy when I ...
7 The saddest/funniest (choose) film I have ever seen is ...
8 Most shops in my country are open from ... to ...
9 The wettest month in my country is ...
10 The most expensive thing I have ever bought is ...
11 You are rich when you have at least ... (say how much money)
12 Name a high building or mountain in your country.

From *Instant Lessons 1 Elementary* edited by Peter Watcyn-Jones © Penguin Books 2000

Teacher's notes

38 The family

Aim	To teach the most common names of relatives.
Preparation	Copy the handout on page 123 – one copy per pair.

Introduction (5 minutes)

Tell the class that you went to a big family event last weekend, for example a wedding, funeral, 50th birthday party, etc. Talk about some of your relatives who were there, for example:
My uncle Bob, my aunt Jane and their two children, my two cousins Paul and Joanna, my parents of course and my grandmother. Oh yes, and my sister's son – my nephew – Peter.
Write the words for various relatives on the board. Ask the class if they know any other words. Add these to the list.

Presentation (20 minutes)

Use the layout of the family tree on the handout (Activity B) to tell the class about the following famous British family (it is the British Royal Family). Draw the tree on the board with the names as you go along.
Elizabeth married Philip. Elizabeth is Philip's wife and Philip is Elizabeth's husband. They had four children – three sons and a daughter – namely Charles, Anne, Andrew and Edward. Charles is Andrew's brother and Anne is Andrew's sister. Their parents are called Elizabeth and Philip. Elizabeth is their mother and Philip is their father. Charles married Diana. Anne married Mark. Andrew married Sarah. Edward married Sophie. Charles and Diana had two sons, William and Harry. Anne and Mark had a son and a daughter, Peter and Zara. Andrew and Sarah had two daughters, Beatrice and Eugenie. William and Beatrice are cousins. Charles is Beatrice's uncle and Anne is William's aunt. Andrew has a nephew called Harry and a niece called Zara. So Elizabeth and Philip have six grandchildren – three grandsons and three granddaughters. Elizabeth is their grandmother and Philip is their grandfather.

Activity A Now give out the handouts and get the students to work in pairs. Check orally.

Practice (15 minutes)

Activity B Divide the class into groups of three to four students. Tell them they have to write in the names of the various people, plus jobs in some cases. Check orally.

Conclusion (10 minutes)

As a final activity, the students use the filled-in family tree from Activity B to play a game called 'Who am I?' One student chooses one of the people in the family tree, then asks the class: *Who am I?* People in the class ask questions, to which the person standing in front of the class can only answer *Yes* or *No*. For example:
Are you Mandy's father? etc.
The class is only allowed ten questions to guess who the person is.

Homework

The students can draw their own family tree.

Key

A 1 father   2 grandmother   3 husband   4 niece
   5 son   6 aunt   7 cousin   8 granddaughter
   9 mother   10 daughter   11 grandfather
   12 sister   13 brother   14 grandparents
   15 uncle   16 grandson   17 children   18 nephew
   19 wife   20 grandchildren   21 parents

B Top row: David, Sally
   2nd row: John (police officer), Paula (nurse), James (journalist), Susan (doctor), Harriet (secretary), Bob (electrician)
   3rd row: Mandy, Samantha (Samantha, Mandy), Mark, Steve, Peter (Peter, Steve)

38 The family

A Complete the sentences below. Choose from these words.

aunt brother children cousin daughter father grandchildren granddaughter grandfather grandmother grandparents grandson husband mother nephew niece parents sister son uncle wife

1 Charles is William's ....
2 Elizabeth is Zara's ....
3 Philip is Elizabeth's ....
4 Beatrice is Edward's ....
5 Harry is Charles' ....
6 Anne is Beatrice's ....
7 William is Peter's ....
8 Eugenie is Philip's ....
9 Sarah is Beatrice's ....
10 Eugenie is Sarah's ....
11 Philip is Harry's ....
12 Zara is Peter's ....
13 Edward is Andrew's ....
14 Elizabeth and Philip are Beatrice's ....
15 Andrew is William's ....
16 Peter is Elizabeth's ....
17 Philip has four ....
18 Harry is Anne's ....
19 Elizabeth is Philip's ....
20 Elizabeth has six ....
21 Elizabeth and Philip are Edward's ....

B Read the clues, then write down all the names, and six people's jobs.

1 Mark is David's grandson.
2 The doctor is married to James.
3 Mandy and Samantha are sisters.
4 Peter and Mark are cousins.
5 Samantha's father is a police officer.
6 The nurse has two daughters.
7 David and Sally have three children.
8 Harriet has two brothers.
9 Paula is Steve's aunt.
10 Bob has a nephew called Mark.
11 Steve and Peter's father is an electrician.
12 Bob's wife is a secretary.
13 John and James are brothers.
14 Susan is married to a journalist.
15 The police officer is called John.
16 Mark doesn't have any brothers or sisters.
17 Sally's daughter is called Harriet.
18 Bob is an electrician.
19 Mark's mother is a doctor.
20 David and Sally have five grandchildren.

Teacher's notes

39 Shops and shopping

Aim	To teach (a) some collective nouns used when shopping (*a kilo of, a tin of*, etc.) (b) different types of shops and what they sell.
Preparation	Copy the handout on page 125 – one copy per pair.

Introduction *(5 minutes)*

Introduce the subject by telling the students that you went to the supermarket on your way home last night and bought the following (write them on the board):
*a kilo of apples   a packet of biscuits
a tin of soup   a dozen eggs   a loaf of bread*
Check that the students understand the above, then add: *I went to the supermarket yesterday and I bought ____ and ____.*
Get one or two student to read out the above sentence and add two items, either from the list on the board or new items. Help where necessary and add to the board.

Presentation 1 *(10 minutes)*

Activity A This activity focuses on some common collective nouns used when shopping. The students work in pairs. Give each pair a handout. Go through the first example with the whole class, then let them work out the rest. Check orally. Then they can test each other. They cover the answer boxes then take it in turns to read out a word on the right (for example, *bread*) and to give the correct reply (*a loaf of*).

Presentation 2 *(10 minutes)*

Activity B This activity concentrates on different types of shops and some of the things you can buy in them. Once again, students work in pairs. Give each pair a handout. Do the first one orally, then let them complete the rest. Check orally.

Practice *(15 minutes)*

This is a simple pair practice based on short dialogues. Write the following on the board:
A: *Where did you buy that/those ____?*
B: *At the ____.*

A: *What did you buy at the ____?*
B: *A/an/some ____.*

Go through both dialogues orally with the whole class. Make sure that they understand that *those* in the first dialogue and *some* in the second dialogue are used with plural words. Let them practice together for about 5 minutes. Encourage them to use collective nouns too (*a tin of*, etc.).
After about 5 minutes, rub out the above and write the following on the board instead:
A: *Are you going to the ____?* (shop)
B: *Yes, I am.*
A: *Good. Could you get me ____?*
B: *Certainly.*
A: *And could you get me ____ too?*
B: *Sorry. I'm not going to the ____.* (shop)
Demonstrate the above, with for example: *baker/a loaf of bread* and *a newspaper/newsagent's*. Then let the students make up their own dialogues. Listen to one or two pairs at the end.

Conclusion *(10 minutes)*

This is a simple check to see if they remember the collective nouns and shops they have been practising. Read out the words below. After you read, ask the students to supply the correct collective noun or shop.
Collective nouns: 1 flowers 2 bread 3 milk 4 apples 5 matches 6 soap 7 wine 8 cat food
Shops: *Where would you buy the following?*
1 a pair of boots 2 a roll of film 3 a table 4 a watch 5 some apples 6 some stamps 7 a loaf of bread 8 a hammer 9 a magazine 10 meat

Homework

The students keep a shopping list for the weekend, writing down what they buy and where they buy it. You can also ask them to write down the five things they buy most often and the five things they buy least often.

Key

A 1 e 2 l 3 f 4 k 5 d 6 h 7 a 8 j 9 g 10 b 11 i 12 c
B 1 clothes shop/boutique 2 furniture shop 3 newsagent
4 sports shop 5 baker 6 camera shop 7 florist
8 post office 9 tobacconist 10 butcher 11 fishmonger
12 ironmonger 13 shoe shop 14 toy shop 15 café
16 chemist 17 greengrocer 18 record shop
19 card shop 20 jeweller

Conclusion
Collective nouns: 1 a bunch of 2 a loaf of
3 a litre/bottle of 4 a kilo of 5 a box of 6 a bar of
7 a bottle of 8 a tin of
Shops: 1 shoe shop 2 camera shop 3 furniture shop
4 jeweller 5 greengrocer 6 post office 7 baker
8 ironmonger 9 newsagent 10 butcher

39 Shops and shopping

A Match up the following. Write your answers in the boxes below.

1	a bar of	a	potatoes, apples
2	a bottle of	b	crisps, cigarettes
3	a box of	c	eggs
4	a bunch of	d	Coke, beer
5	a can of	e	soap, chocolate
6	a jar of	f	matches
7	a kilo of	g	bread
8	a litre of	h	jam, marmalade
9	a loaf of	i	peas, cat food
10	a packet of	j	milk, orange juice
11	a tin of	k	flowers, bananas
12	half a dozen	l	wine, lemonade

1	2	3	4	5	6	7	8	9	10	11	12

B Fill in the missing words. Choose from the following. Use each word once only.

baker   butcher   café   camera shop   card shop   chemist   clothes shop/boutique
fishmonger   florist   furniture shop   greengrocer   ironmonger   jeweller   newsagent
post office   record shop   shoe shop   sports shop   tobacconist   toy shop

You can buy ...   *at the ...*

1 a dress, a jacket   _____
2 a sofa, a bed, a table   _____
3 newspapers, magazines   _____
4 golf clubs, a tennis racket   _____
5 bread, cakes   _____
6 a camera, a roll of film   _____
7 a bunch of roses   _____
8 stamps   _____
9 cigarettes, matches   _____
10 meat, sausages   _____
11 fish   _____
12 a hammer, a screwdriver   _____
13 boots, shoes   _____
14 a jigsaw puzzle, a doll   _____
15 a cup of coffee/tea, a sandwich   _____
16 medicine, make-up   _____
17 fruit, vegetables   _____
18 CDs, cassettes   _____
19 postcards, a birthday card   _____
20 a ring, a watch, earrings   _____

From *Instant Lessons 1 Elementary* edited by Peter Watcyn-Jones © Penguin Books 2000

Teacher's notes

40 Verb + noun collocations

Aim	To teach some common verbs, especially verb and noun collocations.
Preparation	Copy, cut up and shuffle the verbs and nouns on pages 127 and 128 – one set per group of four.

Introduction (5 minutes)

Write the following on the board. *wash your hair* Ask the students to suggest other words you can use with *wash* (*your clothes, the dishes, the car,* etc.) Do the same with the verbs *eat, wear* and *close*. This is to introduce the subject of collocations, that certain nouns seem to go with certain verbs.

Presentation (20 minutes)

Divide the class into groups, four students per group. Give each group a set of verb + noun cards. Tell them their task is to sort out the cards into verbs followed by nouns. Give them the first one, namely *ask a question*, then let them get on with it. Point out that although some nouns can go with more than one verb, they have to choose the one that will enable them to use up all the cards. (The choice of nouns was deliberate, to make the students think more. Although you can both read and write a letter, since you're unlikely to write a newspaper, then the best answer would be *read a newspaper, write a letter*. There are a number of examples like this contained in the list.) Check orally. (See key.)

Practice (15 minutes)

Each group of four now divide themselves into pairs – an A-pair and a B-pair. The As take all the verbs, shuffle them and place them face down in a pile in front of them. The Bs do the same with the nouns. Demonstrate with the whole class first what they have to do. Choose a pair of As and ask them what their top card is, for example *drive*. Tell the class that the Bs now have to suggest a noun to go with *drive*. Choose some Bs to suggest an answer, for example *a car*. (They can either try to remember a word they used in the first exercise or they can think of a new word.) The pair gets 1 point if the answer is correct. The students can ask you to check if they can't decide if the suggested word is correct or not.

Conclusion (10 minutes)

This is a simple dictation to see how many verbs they remember. Tell the students to write the numbers 1–8 in their notebooks. Now dictate the following, allowing them time to write in the missing verbs.
1   Tom went down to the beach to __(bleep!)__ in the sea.
2   Could you __(bleep!)__ this letter, please?
3   How often do you __(bleep!)__ TV?
4   My brother can __(bleep!)__ French, German and Spanish.
5   I __(bleep!)__ twenty cigarettes a day.
6   Do you know how to __(bleep!)__ the waltz?
7   What would you like to __(bleep!)__ – tea or coffee?
8   The teacher asked her to __(bleep!)__ her name.

Homework

The students suggest nouns they can add to the following verbs (to be checked in the next lesson):
bake   cut   draw   look at   make

Key

Introduction
Possible answers:
eat: a meal, a sandwich, a cake
wear: clothes, a dress, trousers, a suit, glasses
close: a door, a book, a shop

Presentation
ask a question; brush your teeth; comb your hair; dance the tango; drink a cup of tea; drive a car; listen to a radio programme; play the guitar; post a letter/parcel; read a newspaper; ride a horse; sing a song; smoke a cigar; speak a foreign language; spell your name; swim in the sea; switch on/off the light; walk in the woods; watch TV; write a letter

Conclusion
1 swim   2 post   3 watch   4 speak   5 smoke   6 dance
7 drink   8 spell

Homework
Possible answers
bake: a cake, bread
cut: my finger, paper
draw: a picture, a portrait
look at: a picture, the view
make: a mistake, a cake, a phone call

126

40 Verb + noun collocations

ask	a horse
brush	the guitar
comb	your name
dance	a car
drink	a question
drive	a letter
listen to	a cigar
play	the light
post	a newspaper
read	a cup of tea

40 Verb + noun collocations (continued)

ride	your hair
sing	in the sea
smoke	TV
speak	a letter/parcel
spell	the tango
swim	a song
switch on/off	a radio programme
walk	your teeth
watch	in the woods
write	a foreign language